UNVEILING THE UNKNOWN

© 2025 Jason A. Solomon, B.Ed All rights reserved.

No part of this publication may be reproduced, stored in a retrieval system, or transmitted in any form or by any means ~ electronic, mechanical, photocopying, recording, or otherwise ~ without the prior written permission of the publisher, except in the case of brief quotations embodied in critical articles or reviews.

This book is a work of reflective nonfiction and creative spiritual writing. While it draws on universal themes, psychological insight, and symbolic traditions, it is not intended as a substitute for professional mental health, medical, or legal advice.

First Edition ISBN: 978-1-7638935-0-4
Cover design and interior layout by Aussie Guys Books
Edited and published by Aussie Guys Books

For permissions, speaking engagements, and upcoming releases, visit:
www.aussieguysbooks.com.au

365 Days of SOUL™ is a trademark of Jason A. Solomon.

365 DAYS OF SOUL
VOLUME 3

JULY
AUGUST
SEPTEMBER

Your Journey Through Time, Shadow, and Spirit

Beginnings are not always loud ~ some drift in underground, like secret springs.

Jason A. Solomon

Titles in Series
365 Days of SOUL

Seeds of Stillness
Volume 1: January – February – March

Origins of Opening
Volume 2: April – May – June

Unveiling the Unknown
Volume 3: July – August – September

Light in the Layers
Volume 4: October – November – December

Welcome to Volume 3

UNVEILING THE UNKNOWN

Your spiritual companion for the first breath of every day

This is the season of soulwater. First, you slip beneath the surface. Then, you soften into the deep. And finally, you rise ~ not as who you were, but as who you've become beneath the waves.

How to Use Your Book

Unveiling the Unknown is the third volume in the 365 Days of SOUL series ~ a tender immersion into the deeper waters of your emotional and spiritual life. These daily entries are crafted to support you as you move through the unseen tides of your soul ~ with presence, curiosity, and compassion.

This is not a calendar. It is not a plan.

It is a current. A rhythm beneath the surface.

A space where your inner world is invited to breathe, soften, and unfold ~ one sacred moment at a time.

This book offers spiritual steadiness, emotional reflection, and soul-deep trust ~ all gently offered in the first quiet edges of your day.

Let these pages find you before the noise does.

Before obligation. Before momentum.

Even before your feet meet the ground.

This is your morning sanctuary ~ a gentle tide pulling you inward, where you can feel before you think, and remember before you react.

For each day:

- A Soul Narrative or Reflective Story ~ to mirror the inner movement of the day
- The Daily Archetype ~ the part of your being rising gently to meet the moment

- Sacred Wisdom ~ drawn from nature, Eastern philosophy, numerology, and spiritual symbolism
- A Reflection Prompt ~ to deepen your inner dialogue
- A Gentle Practice or Embodied Action ~ to anchor your energy in meaning

Read. Breathe. Soften. Begin Again.

Let the words wash over the part of you that's ready to trust. You don't need to finish every page. Sometimes a single phrase carries you farther than a full answer.

Seasonal Awareness: July - September

Whether you're in the Northern Hemisphere entering the inward tides of late summer, or the Southern Hemisphere softening into early spring, this volume honors both the depths and surfacing that come with the season.

Summer invites surrender. Spring invites emergence. Both whisper the same truth: "You are ready ~ even if you don't yet know how."

Each day is a meeting with mystery ~ a chance to return to your inner knowing and let what has been hidden begin to rise.

You'll find stories of courage, surrender, vulnerability, integration, and quiet truth. This is not a time to push. It's a time to feel your way forward.

Why Depth is Sacred?

Before you rise, you must ground ~ not in certainty, but in presence. True grounding isn't about having it all figured out; it's about settling into the truth that already lives inside you, even when it's quiet, raw, or incomplete. Before you speak, pause to listen ~ not just to others, but to the subtle signals of your body, your breath, your inner weather. There is wisdom in stillness, in the moments before movement. And before you arrive at where you're going ~ in purpose, in love, in life ~ you must first return to the place within you that remembers who you are when no one else is watching.

This season is not calling for speed or clarity. It invites trust ~ trust in the unknown, in the tides you cannot yet see, in the unfolding that doesn't follow a straight line. It asks you to surrender the rush to understand, and instead to feel your way forward, with softness and grace. Let these pages be your sanctuary ~ a gentle space to exhale, to feel, to reconnect. Let your emotions move like waves, each one arriving with a message, then passing through. Let your soul speak first, before the world begins asking for answers. Here, in the quiet depth of your own unfolding, you are already enough.

"Growth doesn't always rush in ~ sometimes it gathers quietly, like water finding its way into the cracks you've softened with patience."

Contents

July 1 – The Day of Listening Beneath 18
July 2 – The Day of the Softened Shell 21
July 3 – The Day of Moon-Depths 25
July 4 – The Day of the Unspoken Weight 28
July 5 – The Day of Mirror Water 31
July 6 – The Day of the Fog Veil 34
July 7 – The Day of Deep Remembering 37
July 8 – The Day of Overflow 40
July 9 – The Day of Breathing Underwater 43
July 10 – The Day of Driftwood 46
July 11 – The Day of the Surface Tension 49
July 12 – The Day of Dreamwater 52
July 13 – The Day of the Hollow 55
July 14 – The Day of Cleansing Rain 58
July 15 – The Day of the Floating Bloom 61
July 16 – The Day of the Inner Ocean 64
July 17 – The Day of Echo Waters 67
July 18 – The Day of Fog and Feeling 70
July 19 – The Day of the Inner Night 73
July 20 – The Day of Hidden Roots 76
July 21 – The Day of Gentle Currents 79
July 22 – The Day of Sacred Thirst 82
July 23 – The Day of Emotional Currents 85
July 24 – The Day of the Tidal Self 88

July 25 – The Day of the Whispering Shell 91

July 26 – The Day of the Silent Depth 94

July 27 – The Day of the Waning Light 97

July 28 – The Day of the Midnight Current 100

July 29 – The Day of the Reflecting Moon 103

July 30 – The Day of Returning Light 106

July 31 – The Day of the Deep Reservoir 109

July Reflection: 112

August 1 – The Day of Emerging Light 116

August 2 – The Day of the Whisper Wind 119

August 3 – The Day of Soft Courage 122

August 4 – The Day of the Listening Field 125

August 5 – The Day of Full Presence 128

August 6 – The Day of the Inner Storm 131

August 7 – The Day of the Gentle Shift 134

August 8 – The Day of Sacred Signal 137

August 9 – The Day of Inner Clarity 140

August 10 – The Day of True North 143

August 11 – The Day of Quiet Integration 146

August 12 – The Day of Golden Stillness 149

August 13 – The Day of Inner Space 152

August 14 – The Day of Quiet Fire 155

August 15 – The Day of the Breath Between 158

August 16 – The Day of Rooted Truth 161

August 17 – The Day of the Emotional Mirror 164

August 18 – The Day of Cleansing Waters 167

August 19 – The Day of the Vast Within..................170
August 20 – The Day of Quiet Harvest 173
August 21 – The Day of Soft Uncertainty 176
August 22 – The Day of Full Circle 179
August 23 – The Day of Soul Simplicity 182
August 24 – The Day of Subtle Joy............................185
August 25 – The Day of Letting Gently Go...............188
August 26 – The Day of Dimming Light...................191
August 27 – The Day of Soul Tides............................194
August 28 – The Day of Healing Rain........................197
August 29 – The Day of Emotional Echo 200
August 30 – The Day of Deep Remembering............203
August 31 – The Day of Sacred Closure 206
August Reflection..209
September 1 – The Day of Carried Waters................212
September 2 – The Day of Echoed Wisdom..............216
September 3 – The Day of Soft Power.......................219
September 4 – The Day of Emotional Refuge 222
September 5 – The Day of Honest Openings 226
September 6 – The Day of Soft Illumination 230
September 7 – The Day of Deep Listening 233
September 8 – The Day of the Unspoken Yes...........236
September 9 – The Day of Gentle Completion 240
September 10 – The Day of Soul Transparency 243
September 11 – The Day of Devotional Presence.....247
September 12 – The Day of Soul-Tethering..............251

September 13 – The Day of the Unfolding Self 254

September 14 – The Day of Inner Lightness 257

September 15 – The Day of Sacred Discernment 260

September 16 – The Day of Soft Boundaries 263

September 17 – The Day of Gentle Truth-Telling 267

September 18 – The Day of Inner Harmony 271

September 19 – The Day of Sacred Pause 274

September 20 – The Day of Remembered Grace 278

September 21 – The Day of Equinox Within 282

September 22 – The Day of Seasonal Thresholds 285

September 23 – The Day of Light Rebalancing 289

September 24 – The Day of Echoed Becoming 293

September 25 – The Day of Soul Integrity 297

September 26 – The Day of Inner Restoration 301

September 27 – The Day of Soul-Witnessing 305

September 28 – The Day of Trusting the Tides 309

September 29 – The Day of Sacred Threads 313

September 30 – The Day of Integration 317

September Reflection 321

Notes 326

Your Depth Has Carried You 329

*Welcome to this season of becoming.
Welcome ~ again ~ to yourself.*

July 1 – The Day of Listening Beneath

A story of silence, submerged truth, and the soul's return to what lies below

There once was a soul who only listened to what was loud.

It responded to demands, deadlines, and voices with urgency. It believed that the important things would come with volume ~ that wisdom would knock or shout or crash.

But something was missing.

Not noise. Not motion.

Something softer.

Something deeper.

One day ~ as the Northern summer bloomed loudly, or the Southern sky hung low in cold quiet ~ the soul sat by a body of water. A pond. A bath. A still puddle. It didn't matter. What mattered was this:

For the first time in a long time, it didn't listen for direction. It listened beneath.

And what it heard wasn't words. It was feeling. Faint ripples of forgotten emotion moving just under the surface.

Grief that had been folded. Desire that had gone quiet. Tenderness the soul had once abandoned for strength.

And then ~ a memory returned. It was the sound of its own voice, not from the mouth, but from the chest:

"I'm here. I've been waiting."

The soul didn't speak. It simply closed its eyes and let that soft truth rise.

Not all messages come as lightning. Some truths are water. They seep, dissolve, reshape ~ and finally emerge.

Seasonal Awareness:

🌑 In the Northern Hemisphere, where life is loud and external, today calls you back inward. Beneath the activity, what feelings have been waiting for your attention?

🌑 In the Southern Hemisphere, winter stillness invites emotional presence. Can you sit with yourself ~ not for answers, but for *recognition*?

Archetype of the Day: *The Deep Listener*

This self knows that silence holds story.

It waits, not passively ~ but reverently. It trusts that the most important things are not broadcast ~ they are revealed.

Symbols of the Day:

- A still pond beneath overhanging trees, unmoving, but alive

- Aquamarine, for clarity in emotional communication and peaceful listening
- The High Priestess ~ inner wisdom, intuition, and sacred mystery
- A conch shell pressed to the ear, revealing memory in soundless waves

Reflection Prompts:

- What part of me have I been too busy or afraid to listen to?
- What emotion rises when I stop distracting myself?
- If I listened beneath my thoughts, what truth might I hear?

Integration Practice: Water Listening Ritual

- Fill a bowl or sink with cool water.
- Place both hands in the water. Close your eyes.
- Breathe and ask softly,

"What part of me wants to speak today?"

- Let the answer come not in language, but in feeling.

Journal it. Hold it. Don't fix it ~ just receive.

July 2 – The Day of the Softened Shell

A story of protection, peeling back, and the sacred vulnerability that makes healing possible

There once was a soul who wore a beautiful shell.

It wasn't made of armor or steel. It looked soft from the outside ~ polite, composed, functional. But inside, it had grown rigid.

This shell had been crafted from years of holding it together. It had kept the soul safe ~ from judgment, from heartbreak, from being seen too deeply.

But one evening ~ as the Northern air simmered in golden warmth, or the Southern chill softened the breath with fog ~ something cracked.

It didn't hurt. It didn't break the soul open all at once. It just… loosened.

A quiet moment with someone kind. A single sentence that pierced the mask. A memory that rose not to shame ~ but to *be held*.

The soul felt it. That trembling place underneath the smile. The ache behind the competence. The longing behind the laughter.

It didn't rush to fix it.

It let the shell soften. And for the first time, something sacred happened ~ it was held *while still breaking open*.

Not in shame. In reverence.

Seasonal Awareness:

🌑 In the Northern Hemisphere, July can carry the pressure of happiness. But joy isn't always loud ~ and softness is not weakness. Let the season be honest, not forced.

🌑 In the Southern Hemisphere, protection may feel necessary in cold. But perhaps you no longer need the armor you once did. Let warmth come through ~ even in small ways.

Archetype of the Day: *The Softened Shell*

This self is not broken ~ it is ready. Ready to release the hardened layers. Ready to be touched where it once flinched. Ready to be seen *and* safe.

Symbols of the Day:

- A spiralled shell gently opening, edges worn by time
- Moonstone, for emotional openness and protection through softness
- The Four of Cups, not refusal ~ but preparation for real receiving

— A tide pool, quiet and full of delicate life beneath the surface

Reflection Prompts:

— Where have I grown hard to protect something soft?
— What part of me longs to be seen, even if it's messy?
— What kind of safety do I truly need ~ not to hide, but to heal?

Integration Practice: The Safe Unfolding

— Sit quietly. Place your hands over your heart.
— Whisper:

"I soften, not because I am weak, but because I am safe."

Then write:

— "My shell helped me survive when…"
— "Now I am learning to live without it by…"

Honor what once protected you. Celebrate that you are strong enough to no longer need it.

Mantra for Today ~

"I do not rush my healing. I honor the shell that held me. And I allow myself to soften into truth."

July 3 – The Day of Moon-Depths

A story of inner tides, emotional cycles, and remembering that darkness is not the opposite of light ~ but its rhythm

There once was a soul who thought darkness meant something was wrong.

It rushed to flip the switch, to light the candle, to speak over the silence. It feared stillness, sadness, the slow quiet of night.

But one night ~ as the Northern moon rose full and heavy, or the Southern sky lay soft with winter hush ~ the soul walked by water.

The surface shimmered, but it was the depth that called.

There, beneath the reflection, lived a different kind of knowing.

The moon didn't shine to expose ~ it shone to reveal.

Not everything was clear. Not everything was cheerful. But everything was *true*.

And the soul understood:

This darkness is not danger. It is the place where my hidden emotions rest ~ waiting to be felt.

It didn't run. It didn't rise.

It sat in the moonlight and let the tide come in.

Seasonal Awareness:

🌑 In the Northern Hemisphere, this is a season of light ~ but light can cast the sharpest shadows. Be gentle with what rises today. You don't need to name it, only notice.

🌑 In the Southern Hemisphere, the moon is often clearer in winter. Let tonight be a mirror. What do you see in yourself when no one else is looking?

Archetype of the Day: *The Moon-Holder*

This self is cyclical, not broken. It understands the sacredness of fluctuation. It does not chase constant clarity ~ it trusts the tide to bring what is needed.

Symbols of the Day:

- A rippled moon reflected in dark water, imperfect but whole
- Labradorite, for accessing intuition, dreams, and shadow wisdom
- The Moon card, inviting the unknown, the mystery, and the deeper self

- A crescent carved in wet sand, temporary but intentional

Reflection Prompts:

- What emotions do I only allow in daylight ~ and what comes when the light dims?
- Where have I mistaken stillness for stagnation?
- Can I sit in the moonlight of my life without trying to explain it?

Integration Practice: The Moon Bath
Tonight, find moonlight. If possible, stand or sit under it.
Place one hand on your heart, one on your belly.
Breathe slowly and say:
"I do not fear what is dark. I let the tide rise. I let myself feel."

Journal:
"If the moon could speak my feelings tonight, it would say…"

Mantra for Today ~

"I trust the rhythms I do not fully understand. I allow what rises in the quiet. My depth is not a problem ~ it is a portal."

July 4 – The Day of the Unspoken Weight

A story of invisible burdens, quiet ache, and the sacred relief that comes when we stop carrying what was never ours

There once was a soul who carried a heavy bag.

It didn't remember when it picked it up. Some pieces were old ~ given to them by others. Some were shaped by shame. Some were griefs never named aloud.

The soul carried this weight politely. It smiled. It helped. It functioned. But it began to ache.

One morning ~ as the Northern sun blazed in relentless brightness, or the Southern mist hung low like a woollen veil ~ the soul stopped.

It couldn't carry it anymore.

So it sat down on the earth and opened the bag.

Inside were names that weren't theirs. Stories they were told to believe. Expectations that had never fit. Guilt. Silence. Generational sorrow.

The soul cried. Not because of what was inside ~ but because of how long they had tried to hold it alone.

Some burdens were never ours. Some grief was meant to be released, not rehearsed.

And so the soul, piece by piece, began to lay the weight down.

Not to forget. Not to deny. But to honor it ~ and then let it return to the soil.

Seasonal Awareness:

◐ In the Northern Hemisphere, there can be pressure to appear light and free. But inner heaviness is not a failure. Let yourself be honest about what you're carrying.

◐ In the Southern Hemisphere, winter often reveals old weight we've tucked away. Let this season offer a place to *unpack*. You do not have to carry it all.

Archetype of the Day: *The Burden-Bearer*

This self is not weak ~ it is tired. Tired of being the strong one. Tired of swallowing emotion. Tired of pretending "I'm fine."

Today, it is finally allowed to put something down.

Symbols of the Day:

- A bundle of stones gently returned to river's edge
- Black tourmaline, for protection and energetic release
- The Ten of Wands, not failure ~ but the call to set down what overwhelms
- A wet cloak hung to dry, no longer clinging to the skin

Reflection Prompts:

- What weight am I carrying that no longer belongs to me?
- What was I taught to hold in silence ~ and what happens if I name it now?
- How would it feel to be supported, even when I don't have it all together?

Integration Practice: The Weight-Release Ritual
Find a small stone. Hold it. Speak into it:
"This is what I've carried. This is what I release."
Then place it down ~ on earth, altar, water, or beneath a tree.
Say aloud:
"I no longer hold what is not mine."
Write:

- *"I forgive myself for trying to carry it all."*
- *"I now choose rest, support, and softness."*

Mantra for Today ~
"I release what I no longer need. I do not prove my strength through suffering. I am allowed to lay it down ~ and still be whole."

July 5 – The Day of Mirror Water

A story of reflection, raw honesty, and the healing that begins when we truly see ourselves ~ not as perfect, but as present

There once was a soul who looked into every mirror with judgment.

It saw flaws. It saw lack. It saw versions of itself it believed it had to fix. No mirror ever showed love. Only expectation.

But one morning ~ as the Northern breeze stirred soft ripples, or the Southern frost glazed over still water ~ the soul came across a pool.

No glass. No filter. No distortion.

Just water.

And in that reflection, it didn't see "wrong." It saw real.

A face that had endured. Eyes that had wept and witnessed. A mouth that had spoken truths, even when shaking.

For the first time, the soul didn't correct itself. It didn't flinch. It looked ~ and kept looking.

And what it saw wasn't flaw. It was fullness.

Wrinkled by time. Shaped by emotion. Softened by living.

And beneath the surface ~ a shimmer. A truth: *"I was never supposed to look like them. I was always supposed to look like me."*

Seasonal Awareness:

🌕 In the Northern Hemisphere, light reveals everything ~ and sometimes we judge what we see. Today, let your reflection be a place of compassion, not critique.

🌑 In the Southern Hemisphere, introspection is natural. Let winter's quiet help you see yourself more clearly ~ not with shame, but with sacred recognition.

Archetype of the Day: *The True Witness*

This self does not edit. It does not avert. It meets its own gaze and says:

"I see you. And I will not look away."

Symbols of the Day:

— A mirror in a quiet lake, undisturbed, whole in its imperfection

— Blue kyanite, for truthful expression and self-recognition

— The Queen of Cups, reflective, emotionally mature, and tenderly aware

— A mirror polished by breath, not by cleaning

Reflection Prompts:

— What have I refused to see in myself ~ not because it's bad, but because it's vulnerable?
— What part of me is asking to be seen today, not judged?
— If I looked into my own eyes with gentleness, what would I say?

Integration Practice: The Mirror Offering

Stand in front of a mirror. Look into your own eyes. Say softly:
"I see a soul becoming." "I see someone worthy of care."
Write a letter to yourself ~ from your reflection.
Begin:

— *"I've watched you through everything, and here's what I see…"*

Let it be unfiltered. Let it be sacred.

Mantra for Today ~

"I am not what I feared. I am not who they told me to be. I am who I am ~ and I am worth seeing."

July 6 – The Day of the Fog Veil

A story of not knowing, soft confusion, and the quiet power of moving forward without needing to see the whole path

There once was a soul who hated uncertainty.

It needed a map. A plan. A light at the end of the road. Not knowing felt dangerous. Wrong. Like failure.

But one day ~ as the Northern air filled with warm fog, or the Southern winds swirled in gentle obscurity ~ the soul stepped outside and found the path covered in mist.

No clarity. No horizon. Just three feet of visibility ahead. Panic stirred ~ until something softer arrived: permission.

Permission to not know. To not rush.

To let each step be enough.

"If I can only see a little, I will only take a little step."

And that became enough. Step by slow step, the soul realized ~ it was still moving.

Not toward answers. But toward presence.

And in the fog, it felt something rare: Not clarity, but comfort. Not control, but calm.

The soul whispered, *"I don't need to see the ending to belong to the journey."*

Seasonal Awareness:

🌑 In the Northern Hemisphere, fog can hide even bright days. Let today teach you to trust movement without perfection. You are allowed to keep going ~ even if you don't know where it ends.

🌘 In the Southern Hemisphere, the deep stillness of winter fog asks for gentleness. Don't force direction. Let your path emerge one step at a time.

Archetype of the Day: *The Unseen Traveler*

This self walks by inner rhythm. It listens, not to the future, but to the ground beneath its feet. It does not fear the fog ~ it follows feeling.

Symbols of the Day:

- A winding path covered in soft fog, not hidden, just quiet
- Selenite, for clarity, peace, and energetic movement without force
- The Two of Swords, a pause, a choice without full vision
- A paper lantern in mist, glowing just enough to guide the next step

Reflection Prompts:

- Where in my life am I waiting for complete clarity before I move?
- What small step is calling me ~ even if I don't know the whole plan?
- What does trust feel like in my body when certainty disappears?

Integration Practice: The Fog Walk

Take a short walk ~ outside or in your mind. Before you begin, whisper:

"I move by trust, not by proof."

As you walk, ask:

- "What am I learning in this fog?"
- "What if not knowing is its own kind of wisdom?"

End by placing your hand over your heart and saying:

"One step is enough."

Mantra for Today ~

"I walk slowly. I walk honestly. I do not force the future. I move through the unknown with grace ~ and I am safe."

July 7 – The Day of Deep Remembering

A story of soul memory, emotional inheritance, and the sacred act of returning to the truths we were made to forget

There once was a soul who couldn't remember where it began.

It knew its tasks. Its roles. Its responsibilities.

But origin? Essence? That had been covered ~ by years, by shoulds, by forgetting.

Until one quiet night ~ as the Northern dusk softened the horizon, or the Southern stars broke through midwinter sky ~ the soul sat in silence and asked:

"Who was I before I performed?" "Who am I beneath all I've protected?"

And something stirred. A memory ~ not of a moment, but of self.

It wasn't clear. It wasn't linear. But it felt real. It felt ancient.

The soul remembered joy ~ before it was measured. Curiosity ~ before it was controlled. Tenderness ~ before it was taught to harden.

And in that remembering, the soul wept. Not from sadness ~ but from reunion.

This was not imagination. This was remembrance. The truth beneath the forgetting had never left. It had only been waiting.

Seasonal Awareness:

🌑 In the Northern Hemisphere, reflection in high summer may seem strange ~ but deeper truths often rise when the surface is most bright. Let what's ancient within you come to light.

🌑 In the Southern Hemisphere, winter invites memory. Let today be a reunion with a part of you that got buried, not lost.

Archetype of the Day: *The Rememberer*

This self does not invent new identity. It recovers it. It trusts that what is forgotten is not gone ~ only quiet. It listens to the whispers beneath the noise.

Symbols of the Day:

- A candle lit in front of an old photograph, memory soft and glowing
- Lapis lazuli, for truth, inner wisdom, and ancestral connection
- The Six of Cups, emotional memory, innocence, reconnection
- A spiral carved into stone, ancient and present at once

Reflection Prompts:

- What part of me have I forgotten ~ not because it died, but because it was hidden?
- What did I once know about myself before the world taught me to forget?
- What am I ready to remember ~ not with my mind, but with my heart?

Integration Practice: Soul Memory Ritual

Sit with a candle or image that feels ancient or sacred to you. Breathe slowly and whisper:

"I am returning. I am remembering. I welcome what is real."

Write the phrase:

- *"I used to know…"*
- *"Now I begin to remember…"*

Let it come without proof ~ only feeling.

Mantra for Today ~

"I do not need to invent who I am. I only need to remember. I return to the truth that never left ~ only waited."

July 8 – The Day of Overflow

A story of emotion spilling over, sacred overwhelm, and the healing that happens when we let the flood come

There once was a soul who kept everything tightly held.

It measured its tears. It organized its thoughts. It stayed strong ~ not for pride, but for survival.

But emotions don't disappear. They wait.

And one day ~ as the Northern heat pressed heavy against the skin, or the Southern rain arrived sudden and unannounced ~ the soul cracked.

Not broken. Not shattered. Just... opened.

And through the opening came water.

Tears. Laughter. Anger. Relief. Memories.

It wasn't tidy. It wasn't timed. But it was *true*.

The soul overflowed ~ and the world did not end. No one ran. No lightning struck.

Instead, something sacred happened.

The overflow was not collapse. It was cleansing.

The dam wasn't weakness. It was a gate. And today, the gate was ready to release.

Seasonal Awareness:

🌑 In the Northern Hemisphere, energy builds. Pressure to "keep it together" may feel strong. Today is your permission to *let go*. You are allowed to be full ~ and let it spill.

🌑 In the Southern Hemisphere, rain is part of life. Let emotional rain fall without shame. It softens what was brittle and nourishes what was hidden.

Archetype of the Day: *The Flooded One*

This self is not a problem. It is a truth too big to stay small. It does not break ~ it flows. It does not destroy ~ it heals through release.

Symbols of the Day:

- A river spilling over its banks, no longer contained
- Chrysocolla, for emotional release and authentic expression
- The Ace of Cups, overflowing emotion, spiritual abundance, readiness to feel
- A cup knocked over gently, not spilled ~ just surrendered

Reflection Prompts:

- Where have I held back emotion because I was afraid it would be "too much"?
- What does it feel like to allow my fullness without judgment?
- What wants to be released ~ not explained, but expressed?

Integration Practice: Sacred Overflow

If you feel something rising ~ let it.

Cry. Laugh. Move. Write. Scream into a pillow. Sing to the ocean.

Then place your hands over your heart and say:

"That was sacred. That was allowed."

Write:

- "I overflowed because…"
- *"After the release, I felt…"*

Mantra for Today ~

"I do not hold myself hostage to silence. I am allowed to spill. I overflow with life ~ and that is holy."

July 9 – The Day of Breathing Underwater

A story of emotional survival, intuitive depth, and discovering that what once drowned you can now carry you

There once was a soul who feared the deep.

It knew how to float ~ to stay at the surface of life, of feeling. It kept busy. It kept bright. It kept breathing above it all.

But beneath the surface were memories. Feelings. Things it had never touched ~ only avoided.

Then one day ~ as the Northern skies pulsed with summer heat, or the Southern air thickened with fog and memory ~ the soul was pulled under.

Not by force. Not by accident. But by readiness.

Down it went. Past the noise. Past the stories. Past what it thought it could survive.

And there ~ at the bottom ~ the soul realized something stunning:

It could still breathe.

Not through lungs. Through truth. Through surrender.

The water that once threatened to drown it had become its sanctuary. It didn't panic. It didn't flee.

It listened. It felt. And it discovered:

"The depth I once feared is the depth I now belong to."

Seasonal Awareness:

🌗 In the Northern Hemisphere, July may push toward brightness ~ but don't forget the value of inward descent. You are allowed to be deep, even when the world is light.

🌑 In the Southern Hemisphere, this is the month of emotional truth. What lies beneath your surface is not dangerous ~ it is a part of your becoming.

Archetype of the Day: *The Soul Diver*

This self does not skim the surface. It sinks ~ gently, intentionally ~ into what matters. It knows that real breath happens not in escape, but in full presence.

Symbols of the Day:

— A person floating weightless beneath still water, peaceful and awake

— Larimar, for emotional clarity and calm during transformation

- The Hanged Man, surrender, perspective, trust in the unknown
- A bubble trail rising from below, proof of life beneath the surface

Reflection Prompts:

- What emotion have I feared might "drown me" if I felt it fully?
- What would it mean to stay present ~ even as I descend into deep feeling?
- What part of me knows how to breathe, even here?

Integration Practice: Underwater Breathing

Lie flat with a hand on your belly and one on your chest.

Close your eyes. Imagine yourself under clear water ~ weightless, supported, calm. Breathe deeply and say:

"I trust myself in the deep." "I am safe, even here."

Write:

- "When I sink into my truth, I discover…"

Mantra for Today ~

"I am not afraid to feel deeply. What I once feared will drown me ~ now teaches me how to breathe."

July 10 – The Day of Driftwood

A story of being unanchored, slow transformation, and the beauty that remains after all else has been stripped away

There once was a soul who had lost its sense of direction.

It wasn't despairing ~ just unsure. The tide had changed. The map had blurred. What once felt solid now felt... floating.

The soul resisted. It tried to paddle back to something known. It clung to old identity, old structure, old names.

But the current was stronger.

One morning ~ as the Northern tides pulled from the shore, or the Southern streams swelled with thaw ~ the soul let go.

Not out of defeat. Out of trust.

And it drifted.

Not quickly. Not loudly. But with surrender.

No longer clinging. No longer proving.

And as it drifted, it noticed something sacred: The driftwood wasn't lost ~ it was transformed.

What was once sharp had been softened. What was once solid had been smoothed. What was once rigid now carried stories in its grain.

"I am not broken," the soul whispered. "I am reshaped."

Seasonal Awareness:

◉ In the Northern Hemisphere, midyear can bring confusion. Let yourself drift a little today. You are not behind. You are between ~ and that is sacred too.

◉ In the Southern Hemisphere, the waters run slow and deep. Let this season teach you to soften, not control. You are allowed to be in process.

Archetype of the Day: *The Drifted One*

This self is not aimless. It is *yielding*. It knows that sometimes the most important direction is to let go ~ and let time reshape what no longer fits.

Symbols of the Day:

— A piece of driftwood polished by sea and time, resting at shore

— Petrified wood, grounding, ancestral memory, endurance

— The Eight of Cups, choosing the unknown, releasing the familiar

— A slow-moving river, wide, deep, and unhurried

Reflection Prompts:

— Where am I drifting ~ and what might that teach me?
— What part of me is changing without control?
— If I stopped resisting, what wisdom would be revealed in the waiting?

Integration Practice: The Drift Ritual

Today, do something without trying to optimize it.

Take a walk with no destination. Write without editing. Sit without answering any question.

Say:

"I drift. I release. I trust that I am still becoming."

Write:

— *"What I'm learning while I drift…"*

Mantra for Today ~

"I do not need to hold the shore. I am shaped by the water. And even when I drift ~ I am becoming something beautiful."

July 11 – The Day of the Surface Tension

A story of fragile stillness, emotional restraint, and what happens when we finally allow the drop to break through

There once was a soul who had mastered composure.

It knew how to smile when it was breaking. How to nod when it was screaming. How to hold space for others while silencing itself.

It wasn't a lie ~ it was a survival.

But just like water holds its shape before it spills, the soul had reached its limit.

And one moment ~ as the Northern sun baked a quiet lake into glass, or the Southern wind brushed lightly across a frozen dam ~ something shifted.

A single drop fell.

Not dramatic. Not catastrophic.

Just enough.

The tension broke. And through it came a truth the soul had been holding for too long.

"I'm not okay ~ and I don't have to pretend."

The stillness was gone, but so was the strain.

The soul didn't collapse. It softened.

And for the first time in a long time, it breathed without bracing.

Seasonal Awareness:

🌑 In the Northern Hemisphere, the pressure to "keep it together" can feel amplified. Today, let the smallest expression of truth be your greatest act of courage.

🌑 In the Southern Hemisphere, stillness may be real ~ but check whether it's honest. Still water can hold pain. Let yourself break the surface.

Archetype of the Day: *The Holder*

This self is not weak ~ it's practiced. It knows how to stay calm, but is learning how to be *real*. It doesn't fear breaking the surface ~ it trusts that the water will still hold it.

Symbols of the Day:

— A droplet hitting calm water, disrupting nothing ~ yet shifting everything

— Amazonite, for emotional truth and harmonious honesty

- The Four of Pentacles, holding too tightly, learning to release
- A tensioned bubble, perfect until it pops ~ revealing air and light

Reflection Prompts:

- Where am I holding too much inside?
- What would it mean to let just one honest truth rise?
- What is my relationship with expressing "I'm not okay"?

Integration Practice: One-Truth Release

Today, speak or write one truth you've been holding in. Begin with:

"I've been pretending that…" "But the truth is…"

It doesn't need to be shared ~ only freed.

Close your eyes, breathe, and say:

"I release this truth with compassion. It does not weaken me. It frees me."

Mantra for Today ~

"I do not need to hold everything. One truth at a time is enough. I soften the surface ~ and let myself be real."

July 12 – The Day of Dreamwater

A story of intuition, nocturnal knowing, and remembering that not all wisdom arrives in daylight

There once was a soul who trusted facts more than feelings.

It believed in what could be proven. Named. Measured. Explained.

But the soul was tired. Not from doing ~ from denying.

Each night, it dreamed things that didn't make sense. Symbols. Stories. Floods and forests and whispers it couldn't translate.

Then one night ~ as the Northern moon stretched long across midnight, or the Southern wind rocked the windows in rhythmic sighs ~ the soul stopped ignoring the dreams.

It listened.

And the dreams did not offer logic. They offered *language*.

A kind of knowing that didn't need explanation. A sense of being guided ~ not toward control, but toward trust.

The soul realized: "I've spent years asking the wrong questions."

Instead of "What does this mean?" It asked: "What is this revealing?"

Instead of "How do I explain this?" It asked: "How do I honor this?"

And in that soft surrender, the soul felt something shift. It no longer needed certainty. It followed feeling. It swam by moonlight.

Seasonal Awareness:

🌑 In the Northern Hemisphere, dreams may be intense this time of year. Let them guide you gently. Write them down. Let their language stir something sacred beneath the surface.

🌘 In the Southern Hemisphere, long nights invite deep dreaming. Don't rush to interpret. Let the symbolism arrive on its own rhythm ~ it speaks a different truth.

Archetype of the Day: *The Dream-Tender*

This self trusts the invisible currents. It does not dismiss what it cannot name. It lets the soul speak in images, not just words.

Symbols of the Day:

— A shallow bowl of moonlit water, catching fragments of reflected night

— Amethyst, for intuition, protection, and dream integration

— The Seven of Cups, vision, choice, illusion, and inner truth

- A journal with messy dream notes, sacred in its confusion

Reflection Prompts:

- What recent dreams or strange thoughts have stayed with me?
- What do they stir in me ~ not intellectually, but emotionally?
- What would it look like to honor intuition, even without proof?

Integration Practice: Dream Reflection

Tonight, set the intention before sleep:

"I welcome wisdom in unfamiliar form. I trust what my soul shows me."

In the morning, write the first feeling, image, or sentence that comes.

Even if it doesn't make sense ~ let it be your message for the day.

Mantra for Today ~

"Not all guidance arrives in daylight. I trust what stirs in the dark. My dreams are not random ~ they are sacred messages from within."

July 13 – The Day of the Hollow

A story of emptiness, sacred pause, and discovering that space is not failure ~ it is preparation

There once was a soul who feared the hollow places.

The in-between moments. The dry spells. The gaps between what once was and what might be.

When things felt empty, the soul rushed to fill them. With distraction. With noise. With effort.

But one day ~ as the Northern sun cast long shadows across a still field, or the Southern frost left hollow rings on windowpanes ~ the soul could not fill the space.

There was nothing to do. Nothing to fix. Nothing to prove.

Just stillness.

And at first, the hollow felt like a threat. Then ~ a question. Then ~ an opening.

The soul sat quietly and asked:

"What if this isn't a void ~ but a vessel?"

A place not of loss, but of becoming. A pause that isn't absence ~ but sacred readiness.

The soul no longer rushed. It waited ~ not passively, but with reverence.

And for the first time, the hollow did not feel empty. It felt holy.

Seasonal Awareness:

🌗 In the Northern Hemisphere, fullness can become overwhelming. Step back today. Let space reintroduce you to yourself.

🌘 In the Southern Hemisphere, winter pauses can feel barren. But rest is not retreat. What feels hollow may be making room for something deeper.

Archetype of the Day: *The Vessel*

This self is not desperate. It is listening. It holds space for what's next without forcing it to arrive. It trusts that something sacred grows in silence.

Symbols of the Day:

— A clay bowl left empty on an altar, ready to receive
— Clear quartz, for purification, neutrality, and spiritual clarity
— The Four of Swords, rest, renewal, sacred pause
— A well with no bucket, deep and waiting

Reflection Prompts:

— Where in my life do I feel hollow ~ and what if that isn't wrong?
— What am I making room for, even if I don't know it yet?
— What would it look like to honor space, not fear it?

Integration Practice: Sacred Space Ritual

Find or create an empty space ~ a corner, a room, a blank page.
Light a candle and say:
"This is not nothing. This is space becoming."
Sit quietly for 5 minutes. Let it be enough.
Write:

— "When I stop filling every moment…"
— *"What I notice in the hollow…"*

Mantra for Today ~

"I am not empty. I am open. I am the vessel ~ and I am ready."

July 14 – The Day of Cleansing Rain

A story of sacred release, emotional rinsing, and letting the storm wash what no longer serves

There once was a soul who hated to cry.

It had been taught that tears meant weakness, or loss, or shame. So it held back.

Even when the grief rose. Even when the weight grew. Even when the ache threatened to burst from the ribs.

Then one day ~ as the Northern skies cracked and rain came hard and sudden, or the Southern drizzle settled into the bones like a slow rhythm ~ the soul could hold it no longer.

It didn't wail. It didn't collapse. It simply let go.

Tears came. Soft and honest.

Not because something broke. Because something opened.

"I am allowed to rinse," the soul whispered. *"I am allowed to feel what has waited too long to be felt."*

And as it cried, the earth didn't end. It softened.

The soul wasn't emptier.

It was cleaner.

Clearer.

More whole.

Seasonal Awareness:

🌑 In the Northern Hemisphere, heat builds tension. Let emotional rain come. You don't need to hold it all ~ you only need to feel what is yours to release.

🌑 In the Southern Hemisphere, winter's tears are quiet and necessary. Crying isn't breaking. It's cleaning. Let the sky cry with you ~ and feel less alone.

Archetype of the Day: *The Rinsed One*

This self does not cry for drama. It weeps for healing. It knows that salt water cleanses wounds ~ and clears the fog.

Symbols of the Day:

- A figure standing in rain with head tilted back, not hiding
- Moonstone, for emotional balance and fluidity
- The Star, healing, hope, and spiritual renewal after loss
- A single leaf trembling with rain, heavy, then light

Reflection Prompts:

- When was the last time I let myself cry ~ not for pain, but for release?
- What am I ready to rinse from my emotional body?
- What might be possible on the other side of this cleansing?

Integration Practice: Rain Cleansing

If it rains, go outside or open a window. If it doesn't, run water over your hands or feet.

Say:

"I let this water carry what I no longer need."

Write:

- "Today I let go of…"
- *"What remains after the storm is…"*

Let the release be sacred, not small.

Mantra for Today ~

"I do not fear my tears. I honor them. I cleanse what clings ~ and I rise, washed and real."

July 15 – The Day of the Floating Bloom

A story of resilience, softness, and discovering how beauty rises even from the mud

There once was a soul who felt stuck in the dark.

Everything beneath it felt murky ~ heavy with memory, silted with sorrow, unclear. It looked around for light, but all it could see was mud.

So it paused. Not out of surrender, but out of stillness.

And in the silence ~ as the Northern air buzzed with midseason heat, or the Southern ground softened from slow snowmelt ~ the soul felt a shift.

It wasn't dramatic. It wasn't loud. It was a *stretching*.

A slow, upward motion from somewhere inside.

And then ~ bloom.

A small, perfect lotus.

Not in spite of the mud. Because of it. The soul realized ~ *"Beauty is not the opposite of hardship. It's what emerges when we soften in the middle of it."* The soul no longer fought the mud. It used it.

And what rose from that darkness was not broken ~ it was breathtaking.

Seasonal Awareness:

🌑 In the Northern Hemisphere, this is a time of growth ~ but growth can be messy. Trust your roots, even in the mud. Something beautiful is rising.

🌑 In the Southern Hemisphere, the ground is still cool, but something stirs beneath. Not all blooming is immediate. Let the inner softening be your strength.

Archetype of the Day: *The Bloom-Bearer*

This self is not above pain ~ it is grown from it. It does not pretend the mud wasn't there. It rises because the soil was deep and real and full of memory.

Symbols of the Day:

- A lotus flower blooming on a still pond, roots unseen, petals luminous
- Pink opal, for emotional healing and heart-softened resilience
- The Empress, creative blooming, gentle abundance, rooted softness
- A muddy hand holding a bright petal, both sacred

Reflection Prompts:

- What am I rising from right now ~ and what part of me is blooming because of it?
- What would it mean to trust my growth, even in the mud?
- Where in my life is beauty emerging ~ not because it's perfect, but because it's real?

Integration Practice: Mud and Bloom Journal

Draw or write:

- "What my mud holds: ..."
- "What is blooming from it: ..."*

Place a flower, image, or word on your altar that represents beauty grown through struggle.

Say aloud:

"I honor the mud. I rise anyway. I bloom where I am."

Mantra for Today ~

"My beauty is not in my perfection. It is in how I rise from the mud. I am the bloom ~ and the root."

July 16 – The Day of the Inner Ocean

A story of vastness, soul-space, and remembering that your inner world is deep enough to hold everything

There once was a soul who thought it was too much.

Too sensitive. Too emotional. Too complex. Too… everything.

So it shrank. It compressed. It filtered and flattened itself until only a manageable version remained.

But one quiet day ~ as the Northern coastline pulsed with summer tide, or the Southern shores stood wrapped in solemn mist ~ the soul heard the ocean call.

It went to the edge, expecting to listen. Instead, it remembered.

"This isn't outside me," the soul whispered. *"This is what I'm made of."*

It wasn't too much. It was vast.

Deep enough to hold heartbreak. Wide enough to contain contradiction. Still enough to reflect. Wild enough to move.

The soul stood on the sand and felt it all ~ not as chaos, but as truth.

It no longer needed to be small. It needed to be true.

Seasonal Awareness:

🌕 In the Northern Hemisphere, summer amplifies everything. Let your emotional depth rise like tide ~ not for attention, but for acknowledgment.

🌑 In the Southern Hemisphere, the sea mirrors winter's soul. Be vast. Be quiet. Be moved by your own depth. You don't need to rush to clarity ~ you only need to feel.

Archetype of the Day: *The Ocean Self*

This self does not shrink. It expands. It holds memory, emotion, intuition, and contradiction ~ and it welcomes it all. It trusts that it is big enough for everything it feels.

Symbols of the Day:

- An ocean at low tide, revealing what lives beneath
- Blue lace agate, for peaceful communication and emotional clarity
- The Temperance card, blending, balance, and inner harmony
- A single figure standing in waves, neither resisting nor clinging

Reflection Prompts:

— What part of me have I called "too much" ~ and what if it's exactly right?
— Where am I compressing instead of expanding?
— What does my emotional ocean hold that I've been afraid to explore?

Integration Practice: Ocean Within Visualization

Close your eyes. Place your hand over your belly.
Breathe in and picture an ocean inside you ~ vast, moving, alive.
Say softly:
"I am deep. I am wide. I hold it all with grace."
Journal:

— *"My inner ocean contains…"*
— *"What I thought was too much is…"*

Mantra for Today ~

"I am not too much. I am more than enough. I am the ocean ~ and I am learning to trust my tides."

July 17 – The Day of Echo Waters

A story of emotional reflection, patterns repeated, and the choice to respond instead of react

There once was a soul who kept living the same story.

Not because it wanted to. But because the waters it swam in kept echoing back old sounds.

Each time it spoke, it heard its past. Each time it reached, it met resistance. Each time it softened, it recoiled in fear.

One evening ~ as the Northern moon rippled over a quiet lake, or the Southern wind moved gently through trees soaked in yesterday's rain ~ the soul sat by still water.

It said nothing.

And the water answered back ~ nothing.

No reaction. No distortion. No echo.

Just presence.

And the soul realized: *"I've been speaking to my reflection ~ not the world."*

It had been reacting to echoes. Old hurts. Ancient wounds. Reflected pain.

So the soul breathed. And responded differently.

Not to break the echo ~ but to shift the sound.

Seasonal Awareness:

🌑 In the Northern Hemisphere, patterns rise when energy runs high. Watch what repeats today. Not to blame ~ but to understand what seeks healing.

🌘 In the Southern Hemisphere, quiet reveals reflection. See the echoes that still move through you. You can choose a new ripple at any moment.

Archetype of the Day: *The Reflector*

This self does not judge the echo. It learns from it. It listens. And it chooses whether to repeat or reimagine.

Symbols of the Day:

- A stone dropped in still water, watching the ripple shift the surface
- Obsidian, for truth reflection and protective clarity
- The Judgement card, awakening, renewal, seeing patterns clearly
- A mirror held over water, both transparent and distorted

Reflection Prompts:

— What story keeps echoing back to me ~ and what is it trying to show me?
— Where do I keep reacting to what is no longer true?
— What would it look like to choose a new sound ~ a new response?

Integration Practice: Ripple Repatterning

Draw or imagine a still body of water.

Picture dropping a stone into it.

With each ripple, say aloud:

"I am not my past." "I choose to respond with love." "I make new patterns with presence."

Journal:

— "When I hear old echoes, I remind myself…"
— "Today I will respond, not react, by…"

Mantra for Today ~

"I honor what repeats. I release what no longer fits. I ripple forward ~ not in fear, but in choice."

July 18 – The Day of Fog and Feeling

A story of emotional ambiguity, trusting without clarity, and allowing softness even when the way isn't sharp

There once was a soul who wanted things to make sense.

It liked clean answers. Definite feelings. Clear skies and certain roads.

But lately, everything had become foggy. It wasn't sad ~ but it wasn't happy. It wasn't lost ~ but it wasn't found.

One morning ~ as the Northern fields woke shrouded in warm mist, or the Southern hills lingered beneath low cloud ~ the soul stepped outside into the blur.

It waited for it to lift. It didn't.

So instead of resisting, the soul breathed. And walked forward ~ not by sight, but by sense.

It felt its way through the fog. And in doing so, it discovered something unexpected:

"Even here, I can move. Even in this ~ I am still me."

It wasn't about understanding. It was about trusting presence, not certainty.

The fog was not confusion. It was a cushion ~ slowing the rush, softening the mind, inviting tenderness.

And for once, the soul didn't need to "figure it out." It just felt.

Seasonal Awareness:

☉ In the Northern Hemisphere, this fog may feel internal ~ a haze of middle-of-the-year emotion. Trust what you feel more than what you can prove.

☽ In the Southern Hemisphere, winter clouds the path. Let today be soft, undefined. You are not lost. You are being slowed ~ and softened for a reason.

Archetype of the Day: *The Mist-Walker*

This self does not force clarity. It breathes through the blur. It doesn't need sharp edges to move forward ~ it follows what feels like truth.

Symbols of the Day:

- A figure wrapped in soft mist, standing still and unafraid
- Lepidolite, for emotional balance during uncertainty
- The Two of Pentacles, fluidity, adjustment, presence within transition
- A lantern glowing through fog, not to light everything, but just enough

Reflection Prompts:

— Where am I craving clarity ~ and what would it feel like to just allow what is?
— What emotions exist between "fine" and "broken"?
— Can I honor the fog as part of the landscape, not as a flaw in my path?

Integration Practice: Fog-Walk Visualization

Close your eyes. Picture yourself walking slowly through mist. Say gently:

"I do not need to rush to the light. I walk in softness. I trust the way will reveal itself in time."

Write:

— "The fog teaches me…"
— *"What I feel in the haze is…"*

Mantra for Today ~

"I am not confused. I am moving through something sacred. I honor my fog ~ and I trust the feeling over the fix."

July 19 – The Day of the Inner Night

A story of darkness embraced, unseen wisdom, and learning to rest inside what has not yet become

There once was a soul who feared the dark within.

It kept itself lit with plans. With movement. With words and worries and noise.

Because when the inner night arrived ~ still, vast, and starless ~ the soul mistook it for failure.

"If I can't see anything," it whispered, *"I must have gone the wrong way."*

But one night ~ as the Northern world exhaled under a silent new moon, or the Southern winds hushed into the belly of the long dark ~ the soul didn't run.

It didn't light a candle. It didn't reach for answers.

It sat.

And in the silence, something unexpected stirred ~ not fear, but familiarity.

The darkness was not empty. It was *alive*. Womb-like. Vast. Comforting.

"This is not the end," the soul realized. "This is the soil where something unseen is preparing to rise."

It no longer needed visibility. It welcomed *incubation*.

Seasonal Awareness:

🌑 In the Northern Hemisphere, brightness may mask burnout. Let yourself drop inward. There is wisdom in the dark you've been avoiding.

🌑 In the Southern Hemisphere, the inner night mirrors the outer one. Let this be a time to pause expectations. You are not behind ~ you are becoming.

Archetype of the Day: *The Keeper of Night*

This self is not afraid of the dark. It knows that rest, transformation, and soul growth happen unseen. It no longer seeks to light everything ~ it honors the sacred dark.

Symbols of the Day:

— A dark ocean with no moon, still and powerful
— Black moonstone, for mystery, intuition, and protection in shadow
— The Hermit, solitude, inner light, sacred withdrawal
— A closed seed, hidden beneath earth, waiting

Reflection Prompts:

— Where in my life do I fear the unknown ~ and what if that fear is actually reverence?
— What is growing in me that cannot yet be named?
— What if darkness is not absence, but preparation?

Integration Practice: Inner Night Meditation

Close your eyes in a darkened room. Place your hands gently on your heart.

Say softly:

"I do not need to see to trust. I rest in the unseen. I honor what grows in silence."

Write:

— "My darkness teaches me..."
— *"In the unknown, I am learning..."*

Mantra for Today ~

"I rest in the inner night. I do not rush the dawn. I trust what is becoming ~ even in the dark."

July 20 – The Day of Hidden Roots

A story of unseen strength, quiet preparation, and trusting what's growing beneath the surface

There once was a soul who felt like nothing was happening.

It had been showing up.

Tending.

Waiting.

But there were no signs. No blooms. No breakthroughs.

It questioned its path. Its progress. Its worth.

But one afternoon ~ as the Northern fields shimmered in hazy gold, or the Southern ground held firm beneath a fading frost ~ the soul paused beside a tree.

It saw no flowers. No fruit. Just bark. Just stillness.

And yet, beneath that stillness, life pulsed.

Roots reached deep and wide. Not loudly. Not visibly. But necessarily.

"You can't see the roots," the soul whispered, *"but they are what hold it all together."*

It touched the soil and realized ~ its own life was doing the same. Growth was not always visible. But it was real. And it was essential.

Seasonal Awareness:

🌑 In the Northern Hemisphere, outward growth can hide inner depletion. Take time to check your roots. Are they nourished? Or only pushed?

🌒 In the Southern Hemisphere, you may feel little movement. But roots grow best in quiet. Let your depth develop where no one can see.

Archetype of the Day: *The Root-Keeper*

This self does not perform. It strengthens. It understands that what supports your future must be planted and protected now ~ beneath the noise, beneath the image, beneath the surface.

Symbols of the Day:

— A root system beneath bare soil, intricate and alive

— Garnet, for grounding, commitment, and deep vitality

— The Knight of Pentacles, patience, steady effort, unseen investment

— A sapling bending toward light, supported by deep unseen anchors

Reflection Prompts:

- What am I growing beneath the surface right now?
- Where am I judging myself by what isn't visible?
- What would it feel like to trust my roots, even if nothing has blossomed yet?

Integration Practice: Root Awareness Grounding

Stand or sit with both feet on the ground. Close your eyes and imagine roots growing from your soles into the earth.

Say:

"My growth is steady. My strength is unseen. My roots hold more than I know."

Journal:

- "What supports me, even if others don't see it?"
- "What I'm cultivating in silence is…"

Mantra for Today ~

"I trust the roots beneath my life. I do not need to bloom to belong. I am growing ~ even when no one sees it."

July 21 – The Day of Gentle Currents

A story of subtle motion, patient movement, and learning to let life carry you where force cannot

There once was a soul who believed progress required power.

It pushed.

It planned.

It paddled against the current, even when exhausted.

Because slowing down looked like giving up. And surrender felt like losing.

But one morning ~ as the Northern rivers flowed soft with summer heat, or the Southern streams curved between stone and root ~ the soul stopped.

Not from failure ~ from *feeling*.

It slipped into the current. Not to drift aimlessly, but to trust the motion already present.

And something happened.

Without effort, the soul was moved. Not fast. Not far. But *forward*.

It realized: *"Force isn't the only way. Sometimes, gentleness gets me where striving never could."*

It no longer fought the flow. It listened to it. And it let the current teach a softer strength.

Seasonal Awareness:

◐ In the Northern Hemisphere, activity can become addiction. Let today be unforced. Let life carry you ~ you are not behind.

◑ In the Southern Hemisphere, the slowness of winter is not a stall. It's redirection. Let the season move you quietly toward what's next.

Archetype of the Day: *The Carried One*

This self is not passive. It is perceptive. It chooses surrender not out of weakness, but because it knows when it's time to float.

Symbols of the Day:

— A person lying back in a river, eyes closed, moving slowly

— Aquamarine, for flow, trust, and peaceful momentum

— The Six of Swords, gentle transition, moving through grief with grace

— A leaf drifting on current, guided, not aimless

Reflection Prompts:

- Where am I pushing when I could be listening?
- What current in my life is trying to carry me, if I would just allow it?
- What does it feel like to be supported by motion I didn't create?

Integration Practice: Gentle Flow Meditation

Close your eyes. Picture yourself lying in calm water, being carried.

Say softly:

"I do not need to force what is already moving. I am supported. I flow where I am meant to go."

Write:

- "What carries me today is…"
- *"Where I release control, I discover…"*

Mantra for Today ~

"I release the need to control. I trust the current beneath me. I move with grace ~ and I arrive in peace."

July 22 – The Day of Sacred Thirst

A story of inner longing, emotional nourishment, and learning to ask for what your soul truly needs

There once was a soul who had forgotten how to ask.

It gave. It held space. It made sure everyone around it was hydrated, loved, and held.

But it ignored the dry ache within.

Not because it wanted to. Because it didn't know how to need.

Then one day ~ as the Northern sun blazed against the land, or the Southern frost left thirst hiding beneath skin ~ the soul sat quietly and felt it:

A longing. A parched place. A cry not of desperation ~ but of *truth*.

"I am thirsty," it whispered. "And I deserve to be filled."

Not just with water ~ but with rest. With being seen. With emotional replenishment.

And for the first time, the soul allowed itself to receive ~ not as indulgence, but as essential care.

It drank.

And it remembered:

"I do not have to earn what every living thing is born needing."

Seasonal Awareness:

🌑 In the Northern Hemisphere, summer burns brightly. Don't just hydrate your body ~ listen to the inner parts that are craving rest and replenishment.

🌑 In the Southern Hemisphere, the body may feel chilled, but the soul can be dry. What have you been withholding from yourself, emotionally or spiritually?

Archetype of the Day: *The Thirst-Keeper*

This self knows the ache of overgiving. It honors the longing within and learns to name its needs without shame. It teaches that thirst is not weakness ~ it is the first language of self-love.

Symbols of the Day:

— A cracked vessel being filled with water, drop by drop
— Rose quartz, for self-compassion, receptivity, and heart-healing
— The Nine of Cups, emotional fulfillment and receiving what was longed for
— A cupped hand catching rain, open and worthy

Reflection Prompts:

— What have I needed lately but been afraid to ask for?
— What am I emotionally thirsty for ~ and what would it look like to receive it?
— Where did I learn that my needs weren't sacred?

Integration Practice: Sacred Drink Ritual

Prepare a drink with intention ~ water, tea, or warm milk.
Hold the cup and whisper:
"This is for me. This is nourishment. I am allowed to receive."
Sip slowly.
Then write:

— *"I offer myself nourishment today by…"*
— *"What fills me in this season is…"*

Mantra for Today ~

"I do not apologize for needing. I honor my sacred thirst. I receive what is mine ~ with softness and grace."

July 23 – The Day of Emotional Currents

A story of sensitivity, deep attunement, and learning to feel without being swept away

There once was a soul who felt everything.

It didn't just hear words ~ it felt tone. It didn't just see pain ~ it absorbed it. It carried emotions like weather ~ shifting, swirling, soaking through.

At first, the soul believed this was a problem. Others told it to toughen up. To ignore, to detach, to harden.

But one day ~ as the Northern tide pulled strong along the shoreline, or the Southern rivers rushed through thawing ground ~ the soul stopped resisting its feeling.

It listened.

And in that listening, it discovered a truth:

"I do not need to become the storm. I can ride the current ~ and still be me."

It learned to anchor. To ground. To move with the waves, not against them ~ but not *as* them either.

The soul didn't stop feeling. It started choosing what to carry.

Seasonal Awareness:

🌑 In the Northern Hemisphere, heightened energy may stir emotional overwhelm. Let yourself feel ~ but stay tethered. You are allowed to create boundaries within your sensitivity.

🌑 In the Southern Hemisphere, emotional depth may rise slowly and with weight. Let it come, but let it pass too. You don't need to hold what isn't yours.

Archetype of the Day: *The Emotional Navigator*

This self does not shut down. It learns to sail. It honors feeling without losing form. It knows that empathy is a strength ~ not a sentence.

Symbols of the Day:

- A small boat drifting in a strong but steady current, balanced
- Sodalite, for emotional clarity, self-trust, and conscious response
- The King of Cups, emotional mastery, compassionate boundaries
- A rope tied to shore, flexible but firm

Reflection Prompts:

- Where am I swept up in emotions that may not belong to me?

- How can I stay open-hearted without becoming overburdened?
- What does grounded sensitivity look like for me today?

Integration Practice: Anchor Visualization

Sit quietly and breathe. Visualize a gentle current flowing through you.

Then, picture an anchor in your belly ~ steady, grounded.

Say:

"I feel. I flow. I stay anchored in myself."

Write:

- "Today, I choose to carry…"
- "Today, I choose to release…"

Mantra for Today ~

"I am sensitive, not fragile. I feel deeply, but I do not drown. I move with emotion ~ and stay anchored in truth."

July 24 – The Day of the Tidal Self

A story of return, rhythm, and learning that who you are doesn't disappear when you withdraw

There once was a soul who believed presence meant performance.

It showed up.

It spoke clearly.

It gave its all.

But when it needed to step back ~ to rest, to reflect, to be still ~ it questioned its worth.

"If I'm not visible," it asked, *"am I still valuable?"*

One day ~ as the Northern tide receded in a rhythm older than memory, or the Southern ocean swelled gently along the moon's pull ~ the soul stood by the sea.

It watched the tide go out.

Not in failure. Not in loss.

But as a rhythm. As a breath. As something sacred in its returning.

The soul finally understood:

"I am like the tide. I do not vanish when I pull away. I am simply in motion ~ and I always come back."

Seasonal Awareness:

🌑 In the Northern Hemisphere, energy may rise ~ but you are allowed to ebb. Let your absence be sacred. You do not have to stay "on" to be real.

🌑 In the Southern Hemisphere, the pull inward is natural. Let yourself rest without guilt. You're not disappearing ~ you're restoring.

Archetype of the Day: *The Tidal Soul*

This self does not stay constant. It moves by soul-rhythm, not demand. It trusts that presence is not erased by pause ~ only deepened by it.

Symbols of the Day:

— A shoreline marked by retreating waves, quiet, reflective

— Moonstone, for emotional cycles and intuitive flow

— The Eight of Cups, stepping away to return renewed

— A spiral shell half-buried in sand, waiting, not gone

Reflection Prompts:

- Where am I judging myself for needing space?
- What does my emotional rhythm actually look like ~ and what if that's sacred?
- How can I honor my ebb without shame?

Integration Practice: Tidal Rhythm Journaling

Draw two lines ~ one rising, one falling.
Label them:

- When I rise, I feel…
- When I ebb, I need…

Write under each.

Then say:

"My rhythm is not a flaw. It is a tide. And I am always in motion ~ always becoming."

Mantra for Today ~

"I ebb, and I rise. I return in my own time. I am whole ~ even when unseen."

July 25 – The Day of the Whispering Shell

A story of listening inward, quiet intuition, and the sacred wisdom that echoes when the world goes still

There once was a soul surrounded by noise.

Advice.

Expectations.

Opinions.

The constant hum of other voices trying to define its direction.

It tried to listen. It tried to follow. But the more it tuned in to the noise, the more it lost the sound of itself.

Then one day ~ as the Northern breeze rustled grasses under an open sky, or the Southern coast stood hushed beneath slow-moving clouds ~ the soul picked up a shell.

Not to hear the sea. But to remember the sound of home.

Inside the shell was a whisper. Not loud. Not instructive. Not sharp.

Just a truth that had been there all along.

"This is your voice," it said. *"And it's quieter than you were taught to trust."*

The soul held the shell to its ear, not for answers ~ but for *remembrance*.

Seasonal Awareness:

🌑 In the Northern Hemisphere, the volume of life can drown inner knowing. Let today be quieter. Let the voice that doesn't shout be the one you follow.

🌑 In the Southern Hemisphere, stillness offers space to hear what was always there. Even in winter silence, your soul is speaking ~ gently.

Archetype of the Day: *The Inner Listener*

This self does not seek direction outside. It cups its hand around the stillness and waits. It knows that the deepest truths speak in whispers ~ not commands.

Symbols of the Day:

— A seashell held close to the ear, echoing a memory of something eternal
— Celestite, for inner peace and divine guidance through quiet
— The High Priestess, inner knowing, intuition, mystery
— A child sitting alone with a shell, smiling without needing to explain

Reflection Prompts:

— What inner voice have I been too busy or afraid to hear?
— Where am I mistaking volume for truth?
— What would it feel like to trust what whispers inside me?

Integration Practice: Shell Listening Meditation

If you have a shell, hold it close. If not, cup your hands over your ears.

Close your eyes and breathe slowly. Say softly:

"I am listening. Not to the world ~ but to myself."

Then write:

— "What I hear when the world is quiet…"
— *"What I know, even without being told…"*

Let the answers rise softly. Don't chase them.

Mantra for Today ~

"I trust the voice that whispers. I do not need to be told ~ I already know. My truth echoes quietly ~ and I listen."

July 26 – The Day of the Silent Depth

A story of nonverbal truth, soul presence, and the language that lives beneath words

There once was a soul who kept trying to explain itself.

It used all the right words. It crafted stories, gave reasons, made meaning.

But no matter how carefully it spoke, it never felt fully heard.

Then one still evening ~ as the Northern air held a humid hush, or the Southern twilight came without wind or sound ~ the soul stopped trying to speak.

It sat. It breathed. It felt.

And in that silence, something remarkable happened:

It was not misunderstood. It was *felt*.

Not in language. Not in logic. But in presence.

The soul realized that some truths are too deep for words. They are known only through energy, breath, and the space between.

And from then on, the soul trusted silence ~ not as emptiness, but as its most honest voice.

Seasonal Awareness:

🌑 In the Northern Hemisphere, summer's noise can drown your deeper knowing. Let today be a wordless pause. There's truth in your quiet presence.

🌑 In the Southern Hemisphere, winter invites introspection. Let your silence speak for you. What you can't yet say may still be clearly understood.

Archetype of the Day: *The Silent One*

This self does not force communication. It knows when words distort. It honors the sacred depth where language ends ~ and soul begins.

Symbols of the Day:

- A candle burning in a quiet room, offering light, not answers
- Labradorite, for inner reflection and unseen depth
- The Page of Cups, intuitive emotion, spiritual sensitivity
- A stone submerged just below the surface, still visible, quietly holding

Reflection Prompts:

- Where do I feel the pressure to explain myself?

- What truth in me doesn't want words ~ only space to be?
- What would it feel like to be seen in my silence, not just in my story?

Integration Practice: Wordless Awareness

Spend 5 minutes today without speaking or reading. Sit, walk, or breathe in silence.

Place a hand on your chest and say:

"I am still here. Even without words ~ I am known."

Journal only after the silence. Begin with:

- *"In my silence, I discovered…"*

Mantra for Today ~

"I do not need to explain everything. My presence speaks. I am understood ~ even in stillness."

July 27 – The Day of the Waning Light

A story of letting go gently, natural decline, and learning that release can be a sacred rhythm, not a sudden fall

There once was a soul who clung too tightly.

To effort.

To habits.

To hope that something old would work if it just tried harder.

It feared what would happen if it stopped. If it let go. If it admitted something was no longer meant to continue.

But one evening ~ as the Northern sky blushed and softened into dusk, or the Southern moon thinned in a sliver of silver ~ the soul watched the light wane.

Not abruptly. Not in grief. But in grace.

The day did not die. It dimmed.

And in that dimming, there was space.

Space to reflect. Space to release. Space to say:

"This part is done ~ and I bless it as it goes."

The soul did not fall into silence.

It *stepped* into it.

And in doing so, it discovered ~ that endings can be *beautiful when honored, not feared.*

Seasonal Awareness:

🌑 In the Northern Hemisphere, the days remain long ~ but something subtle is shifting. Let this be a time to notice what is beginning to wane, without panic.

🌑 In the Southern Hemisphere, the darkest nights begin to lift. Still, the slowness remains sacred. Don't rush what is fading ~ let it finish fully.

Archetype of the Day: *The Graceful Releaser*

This self does not fight the end. It bows. It blesses. It trusts that every cycle has a sacred close ~ and that the letting go is not failure, but freedom.

Symbols of the Day:

- A candle burning low, not extinguished, just easing
- Smoky quartz, for gentle release and emotional cleansing
- The Death card, transformation, natural endings, composting the past
- A leaf floating down without wind, silent, soft, whole

Reflection Prompts:

— What is naturally waning in my life ~ and how might I honor it rather than resist?
— Where have I confused letting go with giving up?
— What could it feel like to release with grace, not guilt?

Integration Practice: Gentle Release Ritual

Write one thing you're ready to let go of ~ an old expectation, fear, or habit.

Fold the paper. Hold it gently.

Say:

"Thank you for what you taught me. I release you now ~ with tenderness and trust."

Tear or bury it with care ~ a burial, not a banishment.

Then write:

— *"What this space makes room for is…"*

Mantra for Today ~

"I release without rage. I let go without guilt. What fades with grace ~ feeds what will rise."

July 28 – The Day of the Midnight Current

A story of unseen motion, trust in transition, and remembering that healing often happens in the quiet shift between tides

There once was a soul who thought healing had to be loud.

It waited for a breakthrough.

A fire. A thunderclap of clarity.

But none came.

Instead, healing crept in like a tide at midnight.

Unnoticed. Unrushed. Unannounced.

One night ~ as the Northern coast slept under a sky full of stars, or the Southern hills lay hushed beneath the breath of late winter air ~ the soul felt something different.

Lighter. Softer. Not fixed ~ but no longer aching the same.

And it whispered:

"I didn't even notice I was changing. But something in me… shifted."

Not all growth comes with ceremony.

Some arrives in the middle of the night. Quiet. But real.

The soul realized that its journey didn't need fireworks. It needed trust.

Seasonal Awareness:

🌑 In the Northern Hemisphere, this is a season of heat and distraction. Tune in to the subtle. Notice what's shifting ~ even if no one else sees it.

🌑 In the Southern Hemisphere, the soul's changes may be invisible for now. Trust that the dark is not stagnant. It is slowly, surely, remaking you.

Archetype of the Day: *The Quiet Changer*

This self doesn't rush. It honors every unseen turn. It understands that midnight is not the end ~ it is the hour of *deepest becoming.*

Symbols of the Day:

— A moonlit tide returning to shore, barely heard, deeply felt
— Howlite, for calm awareness and subconscious release
— The Wheel of Fortune, movement without control, cycles turning silently
— A shadow moving under water, seen only by those who look closely

Reflection Prompts:

- What has shifted in me quietly over the past weeks or months?
- Where have I been healing without even realizing it?
- How can I honor the subtle ways I've grown?

Integration Practice: Midnight Motion Awareness

Close your eyes and imagine you are floating on dark water.
Say:
"Even when I sleep, I heal. Even when it's dark, I grow."
Write:

- "The changes I didn't notice at first, but feel now…"
- "My midnight healing has made space for…"

Let yourself be proud of the quiet you've moved through.

Mantra for Today ~

"I honor the healing that happens in silence. I do not need proof to believe in my becoming. Even in the dark ~ I am in motion."

July 29 – The Day of the Reflecting Moon

A story of mirrored truth, inner illumination, and remembering that the light you see in others is often what lives in you

There once was a soul who kept looking outward for wisdom.

It followed teachers. It admired beauty. It celebrated others who seemed to shine with clarity and purpose.

But in its quiet moments, the soul wondered:

"Why don't I feel that in myself?"

Then one evening ~ as the Northern moon swelled into silver fullness, or the Southern sky opened wide above a dark, reflective field ~ the soul stood by still water.

It saw the moon mirrored perfectly on the surface.

Not brighter. Not clearer. Just... reflected.

And something clicked: *"The moon has no light of its own. It shines because it reflects."*

The soul stared at the reflection and realized:

"What I see in others ~ strength, wisdom, beauty ~ is already in me. I recognize it not because I lack it, but because I know it."

That night, the soul stopped searching outward. And started listening *inward*.

Seasonal Awareness:

🌕 In the Northern Hemisphere, full moon energy brings intensity. Use it to illuminate your self-worth ~ not by comparison, but by reflection.

🌑 In the Southern Hemisphere, the quiet of winter can reveal mirrors in unexpected places. Let the fullness of the moon show you your own hidden glow.

Archetype of the Day: *The Reflector of Light*

This self does not seek attention. It shines by remembering that light lives within. It reflects others' brilliance not from absence ~ but from recognition.

Symbols of the Day:

- A full moon mirrored in still lake water, soft and complete
- Selenite, for purity, spiritual light, and clarity
- The The Moon card, intuition, reflection, and emotional truth
- A face lit by moonlight, both seen and seeing

Reflection Prompts:

- What quality do I admire most in others ~ and how might that live in me, too?
- Where have I forgotten to look inward for what I seek?
- What does the moon reflect about my emotional truth today?

Integration Practice: Moon Mirror Ritual

Look into a mirror or reflective surface under soft light.

Say aloud:

"The light I see in others lives in me. What I admire is what I am."

Write:

- *"The truth I'm ready to see in myself is…"*
- *"Today, I let my reflection remind me of…"*

Mantra for Today ~

"I do not chase the light. I remember that I reflect it. I shine because I know ~ and I am known."

July 30 – The Day of Returning Light

A story of reemergence, slow joy, and trusting that what was dimmed is not lost, only resting

There once was a soul who had dimmed its glow.

Not out of shame. Not out of failure. But out of *necessity*.

Life had grown heavy. The world had been loud. And for a while, it felt easier ~ safer ~ to retreat into quiet shadows.

But one morning ~ as the Northern sun crested slowly above the horizon, or the Southern skies blushed with the earliest whispers of spring ~ the soul felt something warm stir inside.

Not a fire. A flicker.

It didn't rush to become bright. It let the warmth spread gently. Quietly. *Willingly*.

And the soul realized: *"I am not who I was ~ but I am no longer hiding."*

The light was returning. Not in perfection. But in presence. It wasn't about shining for others. It was about feeling alive ~ for *itself*.

Seasonal Awareness:

🌑 In the Northern Hemisphere, the tail end of summer brings fatigue. Let yourself reenter slowly. Your energy does not need to be dramatic to be real.

🌒 In the Southern Hemisphere, the light is starting to stretch. Let joy return softly. You don't have to bloom overnight. You only need to open a little.

Archetype of the Day: *The Reawakening Self*

This self does not perform light. It *feels* it. It honors the flicker before the flame ~ the sacred return of warmth after rest.

Symbols of the Day:

— A soft sunrise touching water, not loud, just arriving

— Sunstone, for vitality, positive energy, and inner joy

— The Strength card, quiet courage, inner resilience

— A bird singing after silence, tentative, true

Reflection Prompts:

— What part of me is waking back up ~ and how can I welcome it with gentleness?

— Where have I mistaken dormancy for disappearance?

— What joy am I ready to feel again ~ not for others, but for myself?

Integration Practice: Light-Welcoming Ritual

Step into sunlight ~ real or imagined.

Place a hand on your chest and whisper:

"I welcome what is returning. I trust what is rising in me. I am not behind ~ I am reentering."

Write:

- "The light I welcome today is…"
- *"How it makes me feel is…"*

Let it rise at its own pace.

Mantra for Today ~

"My light returns as I am ready. I do not need to shine all at once. I rise ~ gently, wholly, in truth."

July 31 – The Day of the Deep Reservoir

A story of inner reserves, soul endurance, and realizing that everything you've become is water stored for what's next

There once was a soul who feared it was running out.

Out of energy. Out of ideas. Out of self.

It had been pouring and pouring ~ into others, into effort, into the quiet work of healing. And now, it felt... empty.

But one evening ~ as the Northern heat softened into golden shadow, or the Southern chill began to hint at change ~ the soul came to a hidden lake.

Still. Silent. Vast. No waves. No rush. Just depth.

And something whispered from within the water:

"You are not empty. You are holding more than you know."

The soul knelt. Touched the surface. And felt it ~ the reservoir.

Not visible. Not loud. But alive.

All the lessons. All the softness. All the resilience.

Stored. Held. Ready for what was next.

Seasonal Awareness:

🌑 In the Northern Hemisphere, today marks the threshold between intensity and descent. Pause. Feel the weight of all you've carried ~ and all that remains *within*.

🌑 In the Southern Hemisphere, quiet persistence is becoming strength. You are preparing for emergence. Your soul has not stopped. It has been *gathering*.

Archetype of the Day: *The Reservoir*

This self does not overflow ~ it holds. It does not seek validation ~ it is content in fullness. It knows that capacity is quiet power ~ and what is gathered in silence becomes strength in motion.

Symbols of the Day:

- A deep lake beneath still fog, unseen depth, silent potential
- Fluorite, for clarity, inner wisdom, and stored energy
- The Queen of Cups, emotionally full, quietly powerful
- A water vessel hidden in stone, ancient, unshaken

Reflection Prompts:

- Where have I underestimated my own reserves?
- What have I gathered this month, even if it didn't feel like progress?

- What part of me is quietly ready ~ for whatever comes next?

Integration Practice: Reservoir Recognition

Close your eyes. Visualize a deep, clear lake inside you.

Place your hand over your heart and say:

"I am not empty. I hold all that I've learned. I am enough ~ because I remember what I've become."

Write:

- "What I've stored in me this month is…"
- "What I'm ready to draw from next is…"

Let this become your well of strength.

Mantra for Today ~

"I hold more than the world can see. I carry light, lessons, and life in quiet ways. I am the deep well ~ and I am ready."

July Reflection:

'The Month of Descent and Return'

A sacred review of how far you've flowed ~ even if you've barely moved at all

This month has been a descent ~ not a fall. A movement into the deeper waters of your emotional self.

You have listened. You have softened. You have cried, rested, floated, and remembered. And now, here you are ~ not washed away, but reshaped.

You may not have "accomplished" anything the world could measure. But something sacred stirred within you ~ and that counts.

Still water runs deep. And this month, you've become deep.

And in that depth, you've found something rare ~ the courage to be still, the strength to feel without fixing, and the wisdom to stay with yourself through uncertainty.

You've learned that presence is not a pause in growth, but the beginning of it. This was not a chapter to "get through" — it was a tide to move with. And you did. You are. Let that be your quiet victory.

Journal Invitations:

Reflect on your journey with gentle honesty. You might begin with:

- What did July stir in me emotionally that surprised me?
- What moment of inner truth did I finally allow to surface?
- Where did I let myself feel something fully, without rushing to fix it?

And then:

- What is still dissolving in me?
- What part of me has softened ~ and what has it revealed?

Resonant Days to Revisit:

These entries may echo today's state of being. Let them guide you back inward:

- July 6 – The Day of the Fog Veil ~ for accepting emotional ambiguity

- July 12 – The Day of Dreamwater ~ for listening to subconscious wisdom
- July 18 – The Day of Fog and Feeling ~ for trusting presence in uncertainty
- July 28 – The Day of the Midnight Current ~ for honoring unseen transformation

Practical Integration: "Water in Practice"
This month, water taught us:

- To flow, not force
- To rest, not rush
- To allow, not avoid

Carry these forward with:

- A Daily Water Ritual: Drink a glass of water slowly, mindfully each morning, whispering: *"I honor what moves in me."*
- Emotional Check-ins: Use a 1–10 scale to gauge how "full" you feel. If above 7, take 5 minutes to sit, breathe, and write one emotion you need to release.
- Evening Wash: As you shower or wash your face, imagine the day rinsing away. Say: *"What is done, I now release."*

Final Mantra for July ~

"I have flowed through this month with honesty. I have felt, softened, held, and released. What moves in me is sacred ~ and I welcome what comes next."

August 1 – The Day of Emerging Light

A story of renewal, inner clarity, and choosing to rise without rushing

There once was a soul who had grown comfortable in the dark.

Not afraid. Just quiet. Softened. Soothed by the stillness of the inner night.

But something shifted on this day.

Not a demand. Not a pressure. Just a subtle invitation:

"You may rise now ~ not for others, but for yourself."

The soul didn't leap. It lifted.

Like fog clearing at dawn. Like breath returning after pause. Like light that doesn't blind ~ but reveals.

And what it saw wasn't a new identity. It was a remembered one.

Not "better." Not "perfect." Just *present*.

"I am still me," the soul whispered, *"but something in me has softened into readiness."*

It didn't rush to fill the day. It chose to begin ~ with clarity, not force.

Seasonal Awareness:

🌑 In the Northern Hemisphere, August begins with fullness. Energy may surge ~ but let your motion come from *clarity*, not comparison.

🌑 In the Southern Hemisphere, light is beginning to return. Let it arrive gradually. You are allowed to feel the shift ~ without explaining it.

Archetype of the Day: *The Risen One*

This self does not sprint into the new day. It steps into it ~ gently. It trusts that emergence doesn't mean exposure ~ it means *alignment*.

Symbols of the Day:

— A sunrise just breaking the horizon, golden and still quiet

— Citrine, for clarity, self-worth, and renewed energy

— The Fool card, new beginning, open heart, untethered truth

— A seedling pushing through soil, not in haste, but in wholeness

Reflection Prompts:

— What part of me is ready to rise ~ not because I should, but because I can?

- Where have I mistaken rest for retreat ~ and what is actually renewal?
- What kind of light do I want to begin with today?

Integration Practice: Dawn Presence

Before doing anything else today, stand (or sit) facing natural light.

Place your hand on your heart and say:

"I rise with gentleness. I carry the stillness with me. I begin again ~ in presence."

Then write:

- "What I choose to carry into this day is…"
- "The energy I leave behind is…"

Let this be your soft start.

Mantra for Today ~

"I rise without rush. I begin with presence. I emerge from the dark ~ not to prove, but to be."

August 2 – The Day of the Whisper Wind

A story of subtle signals, soul guidance, and remembering how to listen before you move

There once was a soul who kept looking for signs.

It asked the sky, the stars, the people it trusted:

"What should I do next?"

But the answers never came clearly. No bold lightning. No flashing arrows. Just silence.

Until one day ~ as the Northern air stirred the high grasses, or the Southern trees rustled softly without being seen ~ the soul felt it.

Not a message. A *movement*.

A shift in the breeze. A quiet yes. A gentle nudge, not from outside, but *from within*.

"This is it," the soul whispered. *"The answer doesn't come as a voice. It comes as a direction I already knew ~ but hadn't trusted."*

The whisper didn't explain. It invited.

And for the first time, the soul moved without certainty ~ but with complete alignment.

Seasonal Awareness:

🌓 In the Northern Hemisphere, intensity is all around. Step out of the noise today. Let your guidance come through *quiet feeling*, not pressure.

🌑 In the Southern Hemisphere, the winds begin to shift. Listen to the subtleties ~ your next move is likely already rising.

Archetype of the Day: *The Whisper Walker*

This self does not chase big answers. It listens for small truths. It trusts the inner tug more than outer instruction.

It moves with intuition ~ and walks with stillness.

Symbols of the Day:

— A single feather carried on the wind, effortless, aligned
— Angelite, for quiet communication and connection to higher truth
— The Two of Wands, decision made in soul time, not mind time
— A wind chime ringing gently, direction without demand

Reflection Prompts:

- Where am I waiting for loud clarity ~ and missing the quiet cue?
- What inner wind is trying to guide me ~ if I would only trust it?
- What is the difference between hesitation and inner timing?

Integration Practice: Whisper Listening

Step outside ~ or sit by an open window.

Close your eyes. Breathe in and whisper:

"I trust the quiet part of me that knows."

Let the wind speak to your body, not your brain.

Then write:

- "The small direction I feel today is…"
- *"I will follow this whisper by…"*

Mantra for Today ~

"I do not wait for thunder. I follow the whisper. My next step doesn't need to be loud ~ it only needs to be true."

August 3 – The Day of Soft Courage

A story of quiet bravery, emotional strength, and rising without armor

There once was a soul who thought courage meant boldness.

It imagined swords. Speeches. Standing tall in the center of the fire.

But that never felt like home.

The soul wasn't loud. It wasn't fierce. It trembled more often than it roared.

And so, for a long time, it believed it wasn't brave.

But one morning ~ as the Northern air softened beneath golden haze, or the Southern light broke gently through grey mist ~ the soul did something small:

It told the truth. It rested. It asked for help. It cried in someone's arms. It didn't pretend.

And in that moment, it realized:

"This is courage, too. To not hide. To not harden. To not shrink who I am to make others comfortable."

The soul did not wear armor that day. It wore *honesty*. And it walked forward.

Trembling. Tender. And free.

Seasonal Awareness:

◐ In the Northern Hemisphere, the pressure to perform is high. Let today be about courage in *softness* ~ not appearance.

◑ In the Southern Hemisphere, quiet strength may go unnoticed by others. But your softness is seen ~ by you. Let that be enough.

Archetype of the Day: *The Tender Brave*

This self does not shout. It stays. It softens where it used to stiffen. It meets life with presence, not performance.

It trusts that tears are not weakness ~ they are *movement*.

Symbols of the Day:

- A hand held open instead of a fist, ready to feel
- Rhodochrosite, for self-compassion and emotional courage
- The Strength card (again) ~ not force, but inner fortitude and grace
- A petal clinging to a branch in wind, fragile and unbroken

Reflection Prompts:

- Where have I confused silence with weakness ~ or gentleness with lack of strength?
- What would soft courage look like in my relationships, body, or work?
- What part of me is trembling ~ but still choosing to stay?

Integration Practice: Courage Inventory

Write down three times you've been brave in the past year ~ and make sure at least one wasn't visible to anyone else.

Say aloud:

"My strength is quiet. My courage is real. My softness is not a wound ~ it's a way."

Write:

- "Today, I will honor my courage by…"
- *"My softness protects, not exposes, because…"*

Mantra for Today ~

"I do not need to roar to be brave. I rise with honesty, not armor. My softness walks forward ~ and that is enough."

August 4 – The Day of the Listening Field

A story of presence, attunement, and the sacred act of being fully here

There once was a soul who had always filled the silence.

It spoke when things got tense. It fixed when people got quiet. It felt responsible for everyone else's comfort.

But one morning ~ as the Northern grain fields swayed in slow rhythm, or the Southern hills sat in windless quiet ~ the soul stood in a vast open space.

And for once, it said nothing.

It listened.

To wind. To heartbeat.

To something older than words ~ something that didn't need its explanation, only its *presence*.

And in that listening, the soul discovered a peace it had never found in solving.

"What if presence is the healing I've been trying to provide?" it asked.

So the soul stopped doing.

Stopped managing.

And stood ~ as the field did ~ tall, open, and enough.

Seasonal Awareness:

⬤ In the Northern Hemisphere, August asks for slowing down, even in fullness. Let yourself just *be*. Your presence holds more than your plans.

⬤ In the Southern Hemisphere, as energy prepares to stir again, allow stillness a little longer. What you notice today will shape what you create tomorrow.

Archetype of the Day: *The Attuned One*

This self doesn't rush to respond. It listens. It receives. It understands that being present with others ~ and with oneself ~ is a sacred act of connection.

Symbols of the Day:

— A field of wheat rustling in wind, responsive, not reactive

— Moss agate, for grounding and gentle emotional openness

— The Page of Pentacles, attention to small details, humble presence

— A chair under a tree, unoccupied, waiting without urgency

Reflection Prompts:

- Where do I feel the need to "fix" before I've fully listened?
- What might I hear if I let stillness speak first?
- What part of me is asking to be present ~ not productive?

Integration Practice: Field Listening
Find a quiet place ~ indoors or outdoors.
Sit. Don't do. Just listen.
Say:
"I am not needed to fix this moment. I am only asked to be with it."
Then write:

- "What I noticed when I stopped filling the space…"
- *"What I felt, beneath the noise, was…"*

Mantra for Today ~

"I am present without pressure. I listen without solving. I am enough ~ just by being here."

August 5 – The Day of Full Presence

A story of being seen, felt, and received without shrinking or explaining

There once was a soul who had grown used to holding back.

It dimmed its light. It softened its truth. It shrunk to stay safe ~ even in spaces where it longed to expand.

Not because it didn't want to be known, but because *being seen had once come with pain.*

Then one night ~ as the Northern moon rose round and clear, or the Southern clouds parted to reveal unexpected brightness ~ the soul stood beneath its own fullness.

And for the first time, it didn't apologize for being visible.

It didn't hide behind humility. It didn't mask its joy or mute its knowing.

"I am not too much," it whispered. *"I am whole ~ and I am here."*

The soul didn't seek approval. It simply stood ~ in quiet radiance. And the world, for once, did not shrink from its light.

It reflected it.

Seasonal Awareness:

🌑 In the Northern Hemisphere, this is a time of radiant visibility. Let yourself be fully here ~ not to perform, but to *be received.*

🌑 In the Southern Hemisphere, the days are still soft, but the return of light is felt. Step into that glow ~ even a little ~ and see how it meets you.

Archetype of the Day: *The Whole One*

This self does not shrink to survive. It expands to embody. It understands that presence is not arrogance ~ it is *truth worn freely.*

Symbols of the Day:

— A full moon reflected in still water, undeniable, serene
— Sunstone, for self-worth, leadership, and joyful radiance
— The Nine of Pentacles, self-trust, visible success, unashamed presence
— A person dancing alone in candlelight, radiant with no audience

Reflection Prompts:

— Where have I been dimming my presence to feel acceptable?

- What part of me wants to be fully seen ~ without editing?
- What does it feel like to take up space with love, not apology?

Integration Practice: Full Presence Mirror Ritual

Stand in front of a mirror.

Gaze into your own eyes and say:

"I am here. I am whole. I do not shrink for comfort. I shine from truth."

Then write:

- "The part of me I'm ready to bring forward is…"
- *"I will not apologize for…"*

Let your full presence become your softest power.

Mantra for Today ~

"I am not too much. I am complete. I am full ~ and I am allowed to be seen."

August 6 – The Day of the Inner Storm

A story of emotional weather, sacred release, and finding calm on the other side of truth

There once was a soul who tried hard to stay composed.

It smiled in discomfort. It nodded through overwhelm. It tucked its thunder behind polite clouds.

But beneath the still surface, something stirred.

Then one day ~ as the Northern air thickened with pre-storm tension, or the Southern skies churned with a sudden inner gust ~ the soul could no longer contain it.

Not rage. Not chaos.

Truth.

Raw. Real. And *ready* to be heard.

It didn't scream. It didn't destroy. But it spoke ~ finally ~ without filtering.

"This is how I feel. This is what I need. This is me ~ storm and all."

And when the winds passed, the soul stood clear. Stripped of pretense. Calm, not because it hid the storm, but because it *honored* it.

Seasonal Awareness:

🌀 In the Northern Hemisphere, energy may spike emotionally. Let your expression be healthy. Don't fear the storm ~ it clears what's been stagnant.

🌀 In the Southern Hemisphere, subtle pressures may build. Today is for acknowledging tension before it becomes turmoil. Honor your inner weather.

Archetype of the Day: *The Storm Holder*

This self does not suppress emotion. It listens, releases, and clears space. It trusts that storms, when honored, bring clarity ~ not damage.

Symbols of the Day:

- A tree bending but not breaking in the wind, rooted through motion
- Black tourmaline, for protection, grounding, and emotional boundaries
- The Tower card, radical honesty, emotional realignment, necessary release
- A sky split by lightning, brief but illuminating

Reflection Prompts:

— Where have I been holding back truth out of fear of being "too much"?
— What storm needs permission to pass through me today?
— What might clear if I stop trying to stay composed?

Integration Practice: Conscious Storm Ritual

Write down the feeling that keeps rising in you but hasn't yet had space.

Say:

"This does not make me wrong. This makes me real."

Tear the paper (or speak it aloud privately) ~ then breathe deeply and write:

— "What I feel after the release is…"
— *"What cleared was…"*

Let the air shift. Let it be enough.

Mantra for Today ~

"I honor my emotional weather. I release what wants to move. I clear space for calm ~ by letting the storm speak."

August 7 – The Day of the Gentle Shift

A story of transformation without drama, soft evolution, and honoring who you're becoming without needing to announce it

There once was a soul who thought change had to be big.

It waited for the loud moment. The final breakthrough. The clear sign that something had truly transformed. But it kept waking up… the same. Or so it thought.

Until one quiet morning ~ as the Northern trees whispered in still air, or the Southern sky lit slowly with subtle gold ~ the soul looked back and saw:

It had changed. Quietly. Softly. Invisibly. Not in a single moment. But in hundreds of micro-choices.

A breath taken instead of a reaction. A truth spoken more gently. A boundary held without guilt.

"I didn't see it happen," the soul whispered, *"but I feel it now."*

It hadn't reinvented itself. It had *become* itself.

And no one else needed to see it ~ because the soul *knew*.

Seasonal Awareness:

◐ In the Northern Hemisphere, growth may feel invisible now. Don't discount what's shifting beneath the surface ~ your evolution is unfolding.

◐ In the Southern Hemisphere, gentle change is being seeded. Let the small shifts matter. You are not waiting ~ you are *becoming*.

Archetype of the Day: *The Subtle Transformer*

This self doesn't demand attention. It integrates. It listens for what no longer fits and sheds it ~ kindly. It knows transformation can be tender.

Symbols of the Day:

— A butterfly resting, wings still wet, not rushing to fly

— Chrysoprase, for heart-healing and graceful change

— The Temperance card, gentle blending, inner alchemy, balance

— A thread being tied into new shape, quietly strengthening

Reflection Prompts:

— What part of me is quietly changing ~ even if I haven't fully acknowledged it?

- Where am I evolving without effort ~ just through showing up honestly?
- What would it feel like to celebrate subtle transformation?

Integration Practice: Gentle Shift Inventory

Write three things about yourself that feel *different* than they did one month ago ~ emotionally, spiritually, or relationally.

Say:

"I do not need dramatic proof. I am changing ~ and I see it."

Then write:

- "The soft change I'm most proud of is…"
- *"I will honor my shift by…"*

Let that be your quiet celebration.

Mantra for Today ~

"My growth is not always loud. It is real. I am becoming more of myself ~ one breath at a time."

August 8 – The Day of Sacred Signal

A story of alignment, intuitive readiness, and knowing when it's time to answer the call

There once was a soul who kept waiting for the right time.

It second-guessed every instinct. Delayed every beginning. Questioned every stirring of its own knowing. But the signs kept returning.

A phrase repeated. A door opened. A nudge in the same direction, again and again.

Then one morning ~ as the Northern sun rang clear like a morning bell, or the Southern wind shifted without warning ~ the soul felt it.

Not pressure. Not fear. A resonance. Like something within saying:

"Now. You're ready."

Not ready for perfection. Ready for *presence*. The soul didn't need a complete plan. Just a clear beginning.

So it stepped ~ not into certainty, but into *alignment*.

And the call wasn't outside. It had always come from within.

Seasonal Awareness:

🌑 In the Northern Hemisphere, the days are rich with energy. Let today's invitation rise from *within*, not from the noise around you.

🌑 In the Southern Hemisphere, emerging light brings direction. Tune in to what's been knocking softly ~ it may be time to say yes.

Archetype of the Day: *The Aligned One*

This self is not rushed. It waits for the resonance. It doesn't follow signs blindly ~ it listens for the one that *rings true*.

Then it moves with clarity ~ even if quietly.

Symbols of the Day:

— A small bell ringing in a quiet room, clear and undeniable

— Lapis lazuli, for truth, vision, and intuitive clarity

— The Judgement card, awakening, inner call, soul remembrance

— A key turning slowly in a lock, unlocking what was always meant to open

Reflection Prompts:

— What signal has been returning to me lately ~ not loudly, but consistently?

- What call am I finally ready to answer, not because I must ~ but because it fits?
- What does "readiness" mean to me today ~ and how can I redefine it with softness?

Integration Practice: Sacred Signal Pause

Sit in silence and place your hand on your heart.

Ask inwardly:

"What is calling me today?"

Wait. Don't force an answer.

Then write:

- "I keep returning to this truth…"
- *"The door that feels right is…"*

Say:

"I trust this signal. I follow what rings true."

Mantra for Today ~

"I hear the call ~ and it is kind. I trust the signals that repeat. I begin ~ not because I'm certain, but because I'm ready."

August 9 – The Day of Inner Clarity

A story of seeing beneath distortion, dissolving confusion, and finding truth where the noise once lived

There once was a soul who felt clouded.

Not lost. Just unsure.

Everything felt *almost* clear. Almost aligned. But not quite.

It kept searching for answers ~ through others' voices, books, and well-meaning advice.

But clarity never stayed.

Until one quiet day ~ as the Northern skies cleared after weeks of summer haze, or the Southern sun cut through a veil of lingering winter cloud ~ the soul sat in stillness.

No questions.

No noise.

No search.

And from somewhere inside, the fog began to lift.

Not because something new arrived ~ But because the distractions *faded*.

What remained wasn't brilliance. It was *honesty*.

"This is what I want," the soul whispered. *"This is what I need. And this is who I am ~ today."*

Seasonal Awareness:

◐ In the Northern Hemisphere, clarity is often hidden by over-stimulation. Let today be about stillness. What you need to know is already within you.

◐ In the Southern Hemisphere, light is returning in small, sure ways. Look not for answers ~ but for *resonance*. That's where clarity begins.

Archetype of the Day: *The Clear-Seer*

This self does not look outward for certainty. It removes what distorts, layer by layer. It trusts that when enough noise falls away, the truth will remain.

Symbols of the Day:

— A pool of water stilling after being stirred, reflection returning

— Clear quartz, for truth, energy alignment, and vision

— The Ace of Swords, sharp clarity, inner truth, fresh insight

— A pane of glass wiped clean, what was always there becomes visible

Reflection Prompts:

- Where in my life have I been seeking clarity ~ and what distractions might be distorting it?
- What feels true today, even if I can't explain why?
- What am I willing to see clearly, without flinching?

Integration Practice: Clarity Clearing

Take 10 minutes to clear a space ~ a desk, a drawer, a corner. Do it mindfully, as a mirror for your inner space.

As you clear, repeat:

"As I create space, I create vision. I remove what clouds. I welcome what's true."

Then write:

- "When the noise fell away, I saw…"
- *"Clarity feels like…"*

Mantra for Today ~

"I do not force understanding. I make space for it. My clarity comes ~ not through seeking, but through seeing."

August 10 - The Day of True North

A story of direction, soul-guided choice, and returning to your own internal compass

There once was a soul who had wandered.

Not far. But far enough to forget which way was home. It had followed others' paths. Chased expectations. Stepped into roles that didn't quite fit ~ because they looked right on paper.

But deep down, something felt off.

Then one still morning ~ as the Northern breeze shifted with a cooling edge, or the Southern trees leaned ever so slightly eastward ~ the soul stopped walking.

And listened.

There was no map. But there was a pull.

A sensation. An inner magnetic yes.

"This is the way," it heard.

"Not because it's safest ~ but because it's mine."

The soul didn't sprint. It turned ~ gently, intentionally ~ back toward its own *True North*.

Not a place. A direction. A devotion to walking *its way*.

Seasonal Awareness:

🌘 In the Northern Hemisphere, this season asks for realignment. What direction are you following ~ and is it yours?

🌘 In the Southern Hemisphere, this is a time to set quiet intentions. Let today be about *remembering*, not just moving forward.

Archetype of the Day: *The Inner Navigator*

This self doesn't need a detailed route. It listens inward. It orients by truth, not trend.

It walks in the direction of peace ~ even when it's unfamiliar.

Symbols of the Day:

— A compass spinning, then settling, not perfectly, but steadily
— Blue kyanite, for alignment, directional clarity, and inner integrity
— The Chariot, movement with purpose, aligned willpower
— A trail through a forest, faint but certain once you trust your feet

Reflection Prompts:

- Where have I been walking because I thought I "should"?
- What direction feels like mine ~ even if no one else is going that way?
- What does True North feel like in my body, not just my mind?

Integration Practice: Direction Check

Stand with your eyes closed. Breathe deeply and imagine turning toward your soul's North.

Say:

"I remember where I'm going. I walk in my own truth. I trust the pull ~ not the path."

Then write:

- "My True North is leading me toward…"
- *"I feel aligned when I…"*

Let the next step rise from that place.

Mantra for Today ~

"I am not lost. I am realigning. I walk my way ~ guided by something true within."

August 11 – The Day of Quiet Integration

A story of inner weaving, soulful digestion, and honoring what becomes you after the learning settles

There once was a soul who moved from moment to moment ~ always seeking, always shifting, always reaching for what's next.

It read the books. Took the courses. Reflected. Released. Rewired.

But something still felt scattered.

Then one evening ~ as the Northern dusk folded slowly into calm, or the Southern sky thickened with the hush of deep winter ~ the soul did not add anything new.

It sat. Still. Present.

And it whispered:

"I don't need more insight. I need to let what I've already gathered become part of me."

It breathed. And in that pause, something settled.

Not as a conclusion. But as *integration*.

The lessons became part of its bones. The wisdom entered its walk. The truth no longer needed to be repeated ~ it simply *was*.

Seasonal Awareness:

🌗 In the Northern Hemisphere, this is a time of overflow. Step back and allow what you've already learned to root and rest.

🌘 In the Southern Hemisphere, quiet invites absorption. Let the inner soil settle. You are not missing anything ~ you're integrating everything.

Archetype of the Day: *The Integrator*

This self doesn't chase the next insight. It digests. It lets wisdom become embodiment. It weaves learning into living.

Symbols of the Day:

— A thread being stitched into fabric, not fast, but forever
— Green aventurine, for grounding new growth into the heart
— The Hierophant, inner wisdom made real, living truth
— A pot of tea steeping slowly, flavor deepening with time

Reflection Prompts:

— What have I learned lately that hasn't fully landed yet?
— Where am I mistaking more input for true change?

- What does it feel like to let something become part of me without rushing?

Integration Practice: Weaving the Wisdom

Light a candle or sit in soft light. Think of one insight you've received recently.

Say:

"I allow this to settle into me. I do not need to prove it ~ I only need to live it."

Then write:

- *"The truth I've been carrying that is now becoming me is…"*
- *"I will embody this by…"*

Mantra for Today ~

"I am not unfinished. I am integrating. I let wisdom root ~ and I become whole."

August 12 – The Day of Golden Stillness

A story of contentment without condition, and remembering that peace is not something to earn but something to receive

There once was a soul who only allowed peace after achievement.

It had to check the boxes. Earn the rest. Finish the list. Then ~ and only then ~ it could breathe.

But peace never stayed long. Because there was always more to do.

Then one late afternoon ~ as the Northern sun turned fields to gold, or the Southern shadows stretched just a little shorter than the day before ~ the soul sat down.

Not because everything was done. But because something inside whispered:

"You are allowed to feel peace now. Not when. Not after. Now."

It looked around.

Nothing had changed.

Except that the soul stopped measuring itself against the moment.

And in that release, it found stillness. Not in silence ~ but in *belonging*.

It didn't have to earn this. It only had to let it *in*.

Seasonal Awareness:

🌑 In the Northern Hemisphere, fullness of season can create restlessness. Let today be about sitting inside your own permission to pause.

🌒 In the Southern Hemisphere, the pace may begin to return ~ but you still have time. Let peace arrive before the busyness does.

Archetype of the Day: *The Peaceful One*

This self does not hustle for worth. It remembers that being is enough. It lets the golden stillness wrap around the body like a field of light.

Symbols of the Day:

— A sunlit field at golden hour, not silent, but serene

— Yellow calcite, for joy, grounding, and restful radiance

— The Four of Wands, pause, celebration, peaceful homecoming

— A figure resting under a tree, eyes closed, no need to explain

Reflection Prompts:

- Where am I still making peace conditional on achievement?
- What if I gave myself the experience of contentment now ~ just as I am?
- What would change if I let stillness be success?

Integration Practice: Golden Resting Ritual

Step into natural light, or sit near a warm lamp.

Close your eyes. Breathe deeply.

Say:

"I do not need to do more to feel whole. I allow peace. I receive this stillness ~ without permission from the world."

Then write:

- "The peace I'm ready to feel today is…"
- *"I will let myself rest without…"*

Mantra for Today ~

"Peace is not a prize. It is a presence I welcome. I allow stillness ~ because I already belong."

August 13 – The Day of Inner Space

A story of sacred emptiness, spiritual breathing room, and remembering that space is where the soul stretches

There once was a soul who filled every moment.

Silence made it nervous. Stillness felt like something must be wrong.

So it filled the time. Filled the schedule. Filled the silence with sound, movement, explanation.

But one day ~ as the Northern stars began to bloom in the late summer dusk, or the Southern sky opened wide in pale midmorning light ~ the soul entered a space that echoed.

Empty. Quiet. Unfurnished.

And instead of anxiety ~ it felt relief.

"This is what I've been needing," the soul realized. *"Room. Not answers."*

In that space, the soul stretched.

Not physically ~ but spiritually. It felt the truth of who it was when nothing else demanded it to be anything.

Not lonely. Not lacking. Just open.

"I am not here to be full," the soul whispered. "I am here to feel the wonder of space."

Seasonal Awareness:

🌗 In the Northern Hemisphere, this is a time of sensory saturation. Step away from fullness. Let space become your recalibration.

🌑 In the Southern Hemisphere, emerging activity may tempt you to overfill. Pause. The space *between* is where soul clarity forms.

Archetype of the Day: *The Spacious One*

This self does not fear emptiness. It creates room for breath, being, and unfolding. It knows that something sacred happens in the absence of doing.

Symbols of the Day:

- A wide room with nothing in it but light, expansive and alive
- Selenite, for spiritual openness, purity, and energy clearing
- The Star card, renewal, space for hope, soul expansion
- A sky without cloud or sun, pure, waiting, holy

Reflection Prompts:

- Where am I overfilling my life ~ and what am I avoiding with that fullness?
- What would it feel like to create more space in my day, my mind, or my heart?
- What could return to me if I gave it space to arrive?

Integration Practice: Create One Sacred Empty Space

Clear one surface or small corner of a room. Leave it empty ~ intentionally.

Stand before it and say:

"This space is not absence. It is invitation. I let this reflect what I allow inside."

Then write:

- *"What I feel in this open space is…"*
- *"What I welcome through space today is…"*

Mantra for Today ~

"I do not need to be full to be whole. I create space to expand. My emptiness is sacred ~ and alive with possibility."

August 14 – The Day of Quiet Fire

A story of passion without pressure, inner heat, and discovering the strength of steady burn

There once was a soul who mistook fire for frenzy.

It believed purpose had to roar. That drive meant speed. That to be lit from within, one had to burn fast and bright.

But that kind of flame never lasted. It left the soul exhausted. Ashen. Spent.

Then one day ~ as the Northern air held the shimmer of late-summer heat, or the Southern breeze carried the dry warmth of return ~ the soul found itself near a slow, crackling hearth.

The fire didn't scream. It didn't leap. But it warmed everything around it.

And in that moment, the soul recognized something familiar:

"This is me. I am not the blaze. I am the ember that keeps going."

Passion didn't have to be loud. It could be sustained.

And that fire ~ the one that lives inside, steady and sovereign ~ was more powerful than anything that burned for applause.

Seasonal Awareness:

◐ In the Northern Hemisphere, energy may be overextended. Let today be about *steadying* your passion, not exhausting it.

◉ In the Southern Hemisphere, warmth is beginning to return. Let your inner flame rise without rush ~ let it glow before it blazes.

Archetype of the Day: *The Ember Keeper*

This self burns with purpose ~ but without panic. It holds heat over time. It honors the passion that nourishes, not consumes.

Symbols of the Day:

— A glowing coal nestled in ashes, quietly powerful

— Carnelian, for vitality, creative flow, and grounded fire

— The Knight of Wands, focused motion, passionate direction

— A clay oven warming bread, sustained, ancient, real

Reflection Prompts:

— Where have I been trying to "burn bright" instead of "burn true"?

— What passion still lives in me ~ not loud, but enduring?

— How can I stoke the fire within me without letting it consume me?

Integration Practice: Ember Flame Meditation

Light a candle, or imagine a slow-burning hearth.

Place a hand on your belly and say:

"I carry the quiet fire. I burn with truth, not performance. I sustain my flame ~ gently, endlessly."

Then write:

— "The passion I will tend quietly is…"

— *"I honor my fire by…"*

Mantra for Today ~

"My fire is not for show. It is for soul. I burn softly ~ and that is enough."

August 15 – The Day of the Breath Between

A story of sacred pause, nervous system peace, and honoring the space where one moment ends and the next begins

There once was a soul who rushed from one thing to another.

It didn't mean to.

It just forgot how to pause ~ how to rest *between*.

Between messages. Between decisions. Between the inhale and the exhale.

One day ~ as the Northern wind softened into a midseason hush, or the Southern air held the faintest promise of returning bloom ~ the soul noticed something:

There was space.

Not emptiness ~ but *breath*.

A sacred moment that asked nothing.

Not the past. Not the future. Just a now ~ small and shimmering.

"I don't need to fill this," the soul realized. *"I just need to feel it."*

That breath became a doorway. To clarity. To softness. To the moment where nervous system and spirit realigned.

Seasonal Awareness:

🌑 In the Northern Hemisphere, activity often overrides awareness. Let today be about micro-pauses. The breath between is your teacher.

🌑 In the Southern Hemisphere, the coming stir of spring may feel subtle. Savor the stillness now ~ the breath before blooming.

Archetype of the Day: *The In-Between One*

This self lives in the liminal. It understands that peace isn't at the end of the path ~ it's in the *spaces between steps*. It doesn't rush the moment ~ it breathes it.

Symbols of the Day:

— A feather suspended mid-air, in motion, not moving

— Apatite, for clarity, calm, and throat-space expansion

— The Four of Swords, rest, sacred pause, mental recovery

— A bowl of water still rippling, not from new action, but remembered motion

Reflection Prompts:

— Where in my life am I jumping from one moment to the next without pause?
— What lives in the breath between that I've been missing?
— How can I welcome more pause ~ not as absence, but as presence?

Integration Practice: Breath-Anchor Pause

Pause for three deep breaths today ~ *before* any major activity. Inhale slowly. Exhale longer.

Whisper:

"I honor the breath between. I rest in transition. I do not need to fill this ~ I just need to feel it."

Then write:

— "What I felt in the breath between was…"
— "How that pause shaped my next step…"

Mantra for Today ~

"I live in the space between. I honor pause as holy. I breathe ~ and I begin again."

August 16 - The Day of Rooted Truth

A story of grounded knowing, emotional honesty, and discovering what holds when everything else lets go

There once was a soul who kept changing itself to stay connected.

It bent its truth. Softened its no. Nodded when it meant to speak. Because being rooted in truth had once cost it something ~ love, perhaps. Or safety. Or belonging.

But one afternoon ~ as the Northern trees stood firm in summer's sun, or the Southern soil softened with the earliest thaw of readiness ~ the soul placed its hand on the earth.

It didn't ask for permission. It listened.

And the earth whispered:

"You are allowed to hold your truth ~ and still be held."

The soul didn't need to fight. It didn't need to prove. It simply stood. Rooted. Not rigid ~ but real.

And in that stillness, it discovered that some things don't need to be loud to be *unshakable*.

Seasonal Awareness:

🌓 In the Northern Hemisphere, growth can pull us in many directions. Let today be about *returning* to your rooted clarity.

🌑 In the Southern Hemisphere, truth may stir quietly. Let it rise not as a battle cry ~ but as a grounded remembering of who you are.

Archetype of the Day: *The Root Holder*

This self doesn't cling to truth out of pride ~ it stands in it out of peace. It knows that rootedness isn't resistance ~ it's integrity. It grows quietly, deeply, and without apology.

Symbols of the Day:

— A tree with half its roots exposed, vulnerable, powerful
— Red jasper, for strength, courage, and grounding
— The King of Pentacles, embodied truth, quiet confidence, steady leadership
— A circle drawn in soil, defined not to exclude, but to protect

Reflection Prompts:

— Where have I been bending my truth to avoid conflict or rejection?
— What part of me is asking to be more rooted ~ more real ~ today?

— What does it feel like to trust that my groundedness is not too much?

Integration Practice: Root Line Exercise

Stand tall or sit upright. Visualize a line running from your center down into the earth.

Say:

"I stand in what's true. I root without apology. I can be held ~ even as I hold myself."

Write:

— *"The truth I am reclaiming today is…"*

— *"I will stay rooted by…"*

Let the line of your truth deepen with breath.

Mantra for Today ~

"My truth does not make me unkind. It makes me clear. I root in honesty ~ and grow from there."

August 17 – The Day of the Emotional Mirror

A story of reflection through relationship, the courage to feel clearly, and letting others show you what you haven't yet named

There once was a soul who felt unsettled ~ not because of its own inner world, but because of the people around it.

Every conversation stirred something. Every reaction felt amplified. Every emotion felt… complicated.

The soul wondered:

"Why do I feel so much all of a sudden?"

Then one evening ~ as the Northern skies glowed in the hush of a shifting sunset, or the Southern evening settled into windless quiet ~ the soul looked into the eyes of another.

And it saw itself.

Not literally. But emotionally.

The tension. The tenderness. The truth it had avoided naming within.

"You are not causing this," the soul realized, *"you are reflecting what I already carry."*

It didn't blame. It didn't project. It received. The relationship became a mirror. Not a weapon. Not a wound. A *teacher*.

Seasonal Awareness:

🌑 In the Northern Hemisphere, this may be a season of emotional complexity in relationships. Let each connection become a gentle invitation to self-awareness.

🌑 In the Southern Hemisphere, as you prepare to reconnect more externally, let today be a practice in noticing your emotional responses with clarity and compassion.

Archetype of the Day: *The Reflector*

This self allows emotional honesty. It learns through connection ~ not for validation, but for *illumination*. It sees what relationships reflect back and asks:

"What truth am I ready to feel more clearly?"

Symbols of the Day:

- A lake mirroring the clouds, shifting but accurate
- Moonstone, for emotional insight, empathy, and fluidity
- The Two of Cups, mirrored connection, emotional exchange, sacred reciprocity

— A window fogged from breath, clearing slowly to reveal both sides

Reflection Prompts:

— Who or what has stirred emotion in me recently ~ and what might that emotion be showing me about myself?
— Where have I been reacting instead of reflecting?
— What would it look like to thank the mirror, even when the image is hard to see?

Integration Practice: Mirror Presence Ritual

Sit across from a mirror, or close your eyes and picture the person who triggered you most this week.

Say:

"You are not my enemy. You are my mirror. I receive what you reflect ~ with grace."

Then write:

— *"What I saw in you that lives in me…"*
— *"How I can respond differently next time…"*

Let the reflection become a softening.

Mantra for Today ~

"I do not reject the mirror. I learn from what it shows. My emotions are not against me ~ they are guiding me home."

August 18 – The Day of Cleansing Waters

A story of emotional release, sacred washing, and letting go not for forgetting ~ but for beginning again

There once was a soul who carried more than it realized.

Memories that clung. Regrets that echoed. Stories that no longer fit ~ but had become familiar.

It tried to carry them gracefully. Tried to be grateful. Tried to understand them all.

But over time, the weight turned silent. And the soul began to ache in places it couldn't name.

Then one morning ~ as the Northern rains washed the dust from the day, or the Southern frost melted into running streams ~ the soul stood beneath falling water.

Not to be fixed. Not to be healed.

But to be *cleansed*.

The water didn't ask questions. It didn't analyze. It just moved ~ over, through, and around.

"You don't have to carry this anymore," the soul heard in the current.

And something softened. Something surrendered. Not in weakness ~ in trust.

The soul didn't forget.

It forgave.

It flowed.

Seasonal Awareness:

🌒 In the Northern Hemisphere, summer tension may need a soft release. Let today be about washing what lingers ~ without solving it.

🌘 In the Southern Hemisphere, emotional stillness is ready to shift. Let the water move something loose inside you ~ gently, honestly.

Archetype of the Day: *The Cleanser*

This self does not hold for the sake of strength. It lets go ~ when the letting go brings space. It trusts that what is washed away wasn't a waste ~ it was a chapter.

Symbols of the Day:

— A stream running through the forest, constant and clear

— Aquamarine, for emotional clarity, soft communication, release

- The Six of Cups, memories, emotional healing, letting the past be honored without clinging
- A body stepping into a waterfall, willingly, fully present

Reflection Prompts:

- What emotion, memory, or story feels ready to be released today?
- What am I carrying that no longer reflects who I am becoming?
- What would it feel like to let it flow away ~ not with force, but with grace?

Integration Practice: Cleansing Water Ritual

As you shower or wash your hands today, pause.

Say:

"I release what no longer nourishes me. I thank it. And I let it flow."

Afterward, write:

- "Today I released…"
- *"And what remains is…"*

Let water do what words sometimes can't.

Mantra for Today ~

"I do not need to hold what no longer serves. I cleanse in compassion. I let go ~ and I begin again."

August 19 – The Day of the Vast Within

A story of inner immensity, soul-scale perspective, and remembering you contain galaxies too

There once was a soul who felt small.

Overwhelmed by the world. Pressed by pressures it couldn't name. Diminished by voices, expectations, and the sheer *volume* of everything.

So it shrank. Softened. Tried not to take up too much space.

But one night ~ as the Northern sky stretched wide with starlight, or the Southern constellations shimmered in cold clarity ~ the soul looked up.

And it remembered:

"Everything I see in the sky… …also lives in me."

The immensity. The mystery. The quiet fire.

The soul was not just "in" the universe ~ it *was* a universe.

And suddenly, nothing outside seemed too big.

Because within… was vastness, too.

Seasonal Awareness:

🌑 In the Northern Hemisphere, the bigness of life can overwhelm. Let the night sky remind you: you are more than your stress. You are *expansive*.

🌑 In the Southern Hemisphere, stillness brings reflection. Let today remind you: you are not empty ~ you are *vast*. You do not need to shrink to be safe.

Archetype of the Day: *The Inner Cosmos*

This self does not shrink to survive. It remembers that the soul is spacious, eternal, and quietly powerful. It reclaims its scale ~ not to overpower others, but to fully *arrive*.

Symbols of the Day:

- A spiral galaxy mirrored in an eye, boundless and aware
- Labradorite, for mystical truth and soul perspective
- The Star card, hope, cosmic connection, divine remembrance
- A single person under the Milky Way, not small ~ just part of it all

Reflection Prompts:

- Where have I been shrinking ~ emotionally, spiritually, or energetically?
- What would change if I trusted my inner vastness?

- What would it mean to live from expansion, not contraction?

Integration Practice: Soul Expansion Visualization
Close your eyes and imagine the night sky ~ inside your chest. Breathe deeply and say:
"I am not small. I am spacious. I carry galaxies within."
Then write:

- *"The part of me that is most vast is…"*
- *"Today, I will live from that space by…"*

Mantra for Today ~

"I am not here to shrink. I am here to remember. I carry the stars ~ and I walk in my own light."

August 20 – The Day of Quiet Harvest

A story of soul satisfaction, the subtle return of effort, and learning to receive what you've sown

There once was a soul who kept planting.

Seeds of kindness. Effort. Healing. Hope.

It didn't always see the results. And often, it doubted whether anything had taken root.

Then one golden morning ~ as the Northern fields shimmered with the scent of ripening grain, or the Southern ground loosened under warming skies ~ the soul looked back.

And it saw something.

Not a dramatic bloom. Not a spotlight. But something real ~ something *gatherable*.

Moments of peace. Truer friendships. A steadier self.

"I didn't notice it growing," the soul whispered, *"but now it's here."*

It hadn't been waiting for reward. But what it had sown in quiet devotion had returned ~ in equally quiet abundance.

And this time, the soul did not rush past it.

It received.

Seasonal Awareness:

🌑 In the Northern Hemisphere, this is a time of ripening. Pause to gather what your soul has produced ~ even the small joys. Especially those.

🌑 In the Southern Hemisphere, the earth prepares to open. Reflect on what's ready to emerge ~ and what's quietly making its way toward your hands.

Archetype of the Day: *The Gatherer*

This self does not demand results. It stays close to the process. It knows that every small act of care ~ within or outward ~ will offer a return when you're ready to see it.

Symbols of the Day:

— A basket being filled with small fruit, humble, nourishing
— Peridot, for gratitude, receiving, and heart-based reward
— The Nine of Pentacles, earned grace, soul-grown abundance, peaceful harvest
— A journal filled with completed pages, quietly powerful

Reflection Prompts:

- What have I been planting over the past weeks or months?
- Where is it finally showing up ~ even in subtle ways?
- How can I better receive what I've earned ~ without guilt, without rushing?

Integration Practice: Personal Harvest Inventory

Write down 3 ways you've grown or received something recently ~ emotionally, relationally, spiritually.

Say:

"I allow myself to receive. I have tended my soul ~ and now I gather."

Then write:

- *"The part of my life that is quietly thriving is…"*
- *"Today, I will honor the harvest by…"*

Mantra for Today ~

"What I sowed with love returns with grace. I gather my joy without apology. I harvest gently ~ and I am full."

August 21 – The Day of Soft Uncertainty

A story of living the question, surrendering the plan, and trusting the fog as part of the path

There once was a soul desperate for clarity.

It wanted answers. Direction. A map that showed where everything was going.

But life offered none of that. Just silence. Stillness. And fog.

The soul resisted. Pushed for signs. Tried to outrun the haze.

But one day ~ as the Northern landscape softened into late-summer mist, or the Southern air hovered quietly between chill and thaw ~ the soul stopped.

And in the pause, it noticed something: The fog was not emptiness.

It was *protection*. "*You are not lost,*" it heard, "*you are being asked to feel your way forward.*"

No fast decisions.

No forced certainty.

Just a deeper trust in the moment. So the soul breathed, and whispered:

"I don't know ~ and that is sacred."

Seasonal Awareness:

◐ In the Northern Hemisphere, the weight of decision-making may press you. Let this be a day for softness, not solutions.

◐ In the Southern Hemisphere, early stirrings can confuse direction. Don't demand answers too soon. Let today be about *presence*, not proof.

Archetype of the Day: *The Fog-Walker*

This self does not fear the unknown. It walks by sensing, not by seeing. It knows that not-knowing is not weakness ~ it's the beginning of *wisdom*.

Symbols of the Day:

— A path disappearing into mist, unclear but inviting

— Lepidolite, for emotional balance, uncertainty, and trust in process

— The Moon card, illusion, intuition, navigating the unseen

— A lantern glowing faintly in hand, enough light for the next step only

Reflection Prompts:

- What am I demanding clarity about ~ and can I soften that demand today?
- Where is uncertainty asking me to lean in, not pull away?
- What would it feel like to honor the fog, not fear it?

Integration Practice: Walk with the Fog

Close your eyes and imagine you're walking a misted trail. No horizon. Just breath and footstep.

Say:

"I trust this part of the path. I do not need to see it all ~ I only need to stay."

Then write:

- *"What I'm learning from uncertainty is…"*
- *"My next step, even without knowing the outcome, is…"*

Mantra for Today ~

"I walk the unclear path with grace. I trust what I cannot see. My presence is my compass ~ and that is enough."

August 22 – The Day of Full Circle

A story of return, reflection, and realizing you are standing in the very place you once longed for

There once was a soul who always looked ahead.

To the next healing.

The next level.

The next beginning.

It kept moving forward, certain that someday it would *arrive*. But arrival never looked the way it imagined.

Then one soft evening ~ as the Northern light began its golden descent, or the Southern breeze shifted with a hint of bloom ~ the soul paused.

And it noticed where it was. Not in a perfect place. Not at the finish line. But somewhere strangely familiar ~ and peaceful.

It had come full circle. Not by going back. But by *growing* into the very thing it once needed.

"I used to dream of this moment," the soul whispered. *"And now I'm living it ~ not as a goal, but as grace."*

It realized: arrival isn't a destination. It's a recognition. And sometimes the greatest progress is a quiet *return* ~ to yourself.

Seasonal Awareness:

🌓 In the Northern Hemisphere, the season bends toward reflection. Let today be about honoring how far you've come ~ even if it doesn't look like you expected.

🌓 In the Southern Hemisphere, you are close to new emergence. But before you step ahead, acknowledge what you've circled back to ~ gently, intentionally.

Archetype of the Day: *The Returner*

This self does not chase completion. It honors the spiral, the rhythm, the sacred loop. It understands that life moves in circles ~ and that returning does not mean repeating.

Symbols of the Day:

— A spiral drawn in sand, wide, soft, continuous
— Moonstone, for cyclical wisdom, inner memory, sacred return
— The World card, wholeness, completion, the return to self
— A seed planted at the start of the year ~ now blooming, quietly witnessed

Reflection Prompts:

— What part of my life has come full circle ~ even if I didn't notice until now?
— Where have I become the version of myself I once longed to be?
— What would it mean to pause ~ and receive the moment, rather than race ahead?

Integration Practice: Circle Ritual

Draw a circle on paper. In the center, write one way you've returned to yourself. Around the outside, write the steps that brought you here.

Say:

"I do not chase endings. I honor my return. I am home ~ not in place, but in presence."

Then write:

— *"The version of me I've returned to is…"*
— *"And this time, I stay."*

Mantra for Today ~

"I arrive without striving. I return without regret. I come full circle ~ and I remember who I've become."

August 23 – The Day of Soul Simplicity

A story of uncluttering the spirit, remembering what really matters, and letting enough be enough

There once was a soul who had gathered too much.

Not things, exactly ~ but thoughts.

Expectations. Roles. Plans.

Its heart felt cluttered. Its joy, distant. And even in moments of peace, it couldn't settle ~ because something always needed fixing, perfecting, proving.

Then one golden morning ~ as the Northern sun illuminated every line of the harvest fields, or the Southern air turned crisp and present ~ the soul sat with a single cup of tea.

No goal. No improvement.

Just a moment. Just *this*.

And in that pause, something sacred returned:

"This is it," the soul whispered. *"Enough. Right here. As it is."*

The soul had not been missing a breakthrough. It had been missing presence.

And today, it reclaimed the art of *simple sacredness.*

Seasonal Awareness:

🌓 In the Northern Hemisphere, fullness can turn into excess. Let this be a day of gentle subtraction ~ to rediscover what's truly meaningful.

🌑 In the Southern Hemisphere, the impulse to start anew may rise. Begin instead by clearing ~ not adding. Let simplicity lead you into clarity.

Archetype of the Day: *The Sacred Simplifier*

This self does not chase more. It edits gently. It honors what matters ~ not by doing everything, but by doing the *right things* with presence.

Symbols of the Day:

- A single candle on an empty table, whole and enough
- Clear quartz, for purification, clarity, and spiritual focus
- The Four of Pentacles, healthy boundaries, intentional holding
- A bowl with one perfect fruit, chosen, offered, received

Reflection Prompts:

- Where has complexity crept into my life or mind?
- What is truly nourishing me ~ and what is simply noise?
- What would it feel like to choose simplicity as an act of devotion?

Integration Practice: Soul Edit

Write down five things currently taking your attention. Cross out three that don't serve your peace right now.

Say:

"I choose space over noise. I release what I don't need. I return to what matters."

Then write:

- *"The simplicity I will protect today is…"*
- *"When I simplify, I feel…"*

Mantra for Today ~

"I do not need more to be whole. I do not need noise to be valuable. I return to the sacred ~ by choosing less with love."

August 24 – The Day of Subtle Joy

A story of quiet delight, soul-level contentment, and remembering that joy doesn't always have to shout to be real

There once was a soul who kept looking for fireworks.

It wanted joy to be loud. Big. Undeniable.

The kind of joy that turned heads. That made everyone see: *"I'm doing it right."*

But the louder it searched, the emptier it felt.

Then one gentle morning ~ as the Northern breeze danced through tall grass, or the Southern sun filtered softly through fresh leaves ~ the soul heard something small:

Laughter from across a fence. A bird resting, not flying. A single piece of fruit ripening unnoticed.

And the soul smiled ~ not wide, but *real*.

"This is it," it thought. *"Joy isn't always wild. Sometimes, it's tender ~ and asks only to be received."*

That day, the soul didn't chase anything. It simply noticed what was already beautiful. And in doing so, it remembered:

"Subtle joy is sacred joy."

Seasonal Awareness:

🌕 In the Northern Hemisphere, as activity peaks, allow yourself to be nourished by small beauty. Let today's joy be unforced and *felt*.

🌑 In the Southern Hemisphere, new beginnings are forming. Tune into gentle moments that spark softness. You don't need fanfare to feel full.

Archetype of the Day: *The Quiet Bloom*

This self finds delight not in spectacle ~ but in *being awake to the now*. It treasures whispers of joy, not because they impress ~ but because they *connect*.

Symbols of the Day:

— A wildflower blooming at the edge of a sidewalk, unnoticed, full of life
— Pink opal, for heart-softening, tender joy, and emotional sweetness
— The Page of Cups, youthful wonder, emotional presence, unexpected beauty
— A warm cup held between hands, shared with no rush

Reflection Prompts:

- Where in my life does joy speak softly ~ and am I listening?
- What makes me smile in secret, even if no one else notices?
- How can I welcome joy today without trying to earn it?

Integration Practice: Joy Noticing

Set a timer for three moments today to pause and notice one small joy ~ a scent, a sound, a texture, a glance.

Say:

"I do not wait for joy. I welcome it ~ even when it whispers."

Then write:

- *"Today, subtle joy found me in…"*
- *"This tells me my soul is alive because…"*

Mantra for Today ~

"I do not need grand gestures to feel joy. I am awake to the quiet good. I delight in the gentle ~ and it delights in me."

August 25 - The Day of Letting Gently Go

A story of graceful release, soul maturity, and learning that not every ending is an absence ~ some are sacred returns

There once was a soul who feared goodbye.

Even to small things. A habit. A version of self. A dream that once brought comfort. It clung ~ not out of desperation, but because it *cared*.

Letting go felt too final. Too cold.

But one afternoon ~ as the Northern leaves began to curl at the edges, or the Southern buds reached upward through softened earth ~ the soul held a dry leaf in its hand.

It didn't rip. It didn't crumble. It simply *released*. The soul watched it drift. And something inside whispered:

"This, too, is part of the cycle." Letting go wasn't rejection. It was reverence.

"I don't have to hold what no longer holds me."

The soul didn't feel lighter. It felt clearer. And clarity ~ that quiet knowing ~ was enough.

Seasonal Awareness:

🌗 In the Northern Hemisphere, the early hints of autumn ask for gentle inventory. Let go of what's ready to fall ~ not with urgency, but with care.

🌒 In the Southern Hemisphere, you may feel a soft upward pull. What you release now makes space for deeper alignment with what's next.

Archetype of the Day: *The Gentle Releaser*

This self does not rush to shed ~ but neither does it grip. It listens for when the holding is done. It trusts that letting go is a sacred continuation ~ not a failure.

Symbols of the Day:

- A leaf floating slowly in water, released, carried
- Smoky quartz, for grounding, emotional clearing, and release
- The Eight of Cups, walking away with reverence, not regret
- A door left open, no force, just an invitation to shift

Reflection Prompts:

- What in my life feels like it's asking to be released ~ even if I still love it?
- What fear do I hold about letting go ~ and what truth might live beneath it?
- What space could open in me if I allowed this to pass, gently?

Integration Practice: Sacred Goodbye Ritual

Write a short letter to something you're ready to release ~ a pattern, relationship, role, or belief.

Read it aloud. Then whisper:

"Thank you. I release you. I carry your gifts ~ but not your weight."

Write:

- "As I let go, I make space for…"
- *"This letting go is not a loss ~ it is…"*

Mantra for Today ~

"I release with grace. I do not hold what no longer holds me. I let go ~ and I make space for soul to grow."

August 26 – The Day of Dimming Light

A story of quiet descent, sacred dusk, and learning how to soften into the endings without rushing into the next beginning

There once was a soul who feared fading.

It equated slowing down with being forgotten. It equated quietness with invisibility. So it kept shining. Kept striving. Kept performing light ~ even when it was tired.

But one evening ~ as the Northern sky ripened into that deep, golden blue, or the Southern twilight curled softly around the final hour ~ the soul didn't reach for more.

It sat in the soft dim. And for the first time, it noticed something:

"This... is not a decline. It's a return."

A return to pace. To presence. To being *enough* without producing.

The soul watched the day dissolve. And it breathed ~ not in loss, but in *reverence*.

"I don't have to shine all the time," it whispered. *"Some light is meant to dim ~ not to disappear, but to deepen."*

Seasonal Awareness:

🌑 In the Northern Hemisphere, this is a season of slow descent. Honor the dimming ~ let it be sacred, not sad.

🌘 In the Southern Hemisphere, the light is returning, but gently. Let dusk teach you that becoming brighter doesn't mean becoming busier.

Archetype of the Day: *The Dusk Dweller*

This self knows how to rest before the rest is forced. It lets energy taper. It does not race to stay visible ~ it sinks into quiet grace.

Symbols of the Day:

- A sky turning navy at the edges, dusk softening all sharpness
- Lepidolite, for emotional balance, gentleness, and transition
- The Hermit card, inner retreat, sacred solitude, soft illumination
- A single candle slowly burning lower, not extinguished ~ simply offering less, with meaning

Reflection Prompts:

- Where in my life am I afraid to slow down ~ and what truth might live in the pause?
- What would it feel like to dim, not disappear ~ to be quieter, and still valuable?
- What part of me is ready to enter dusk, not as an end, but as a depth?

Integration Practice: Dusk Embrace

Sit in a dimly lit space ~ or watch the evening arrive.

Say:

"I welcome the slow fade. I honor the in-between. My presence does not depend on performance."

Then write:

- "The part of me that softens in the dim is…"
- *"I will let dusk teach me about…"*

Mantra for Today ~

"I do not fear the dimming. I do not resist the hush. I let the light soften ~ and I return to what's real."

August 27 – The Day of Soul Tides

A story of rhythm, emotional return, and remembering that what rises and falls is still whole

There once was a soul who felt inconsistent.

Some days it overflowed with clarity, connection, and confidence. Other days, it withdrew. Doubt crept in. Stillness took over.

It began to wonder if something was wrong. If this back-and-forth meant failure. If steadiness was something it lacked.

But one evening ~ as the Northern waves rolled in with moonlit rhythm, or the Southern sea retreated just far enough to reveal new shells ~ the soul watched the tide.

It noticed something:

"The ocean doesn't apologize for its rhythm."

It doesn't panic when it recedes. It doesn't brag when it surges.

It *returns*. And in that return is a sacred truth:

"I can be full and empty ~ and still be whole."

The soul smiled. It wasn't broken. It was *tidal*.

And that was its strength.

Seasonal Awareness:

🌑 In the Northern Hemisphere, the rhythm of rest and rise becomes more visible. Let your emotions follow their tide ~ with grace, not judgment.

🌑 In the Southern Hemisphere, as life stirs again, remember: not every rise is meant to be held. Let your energy ebb when needed.

Archetype of the Day: *The Tidal Self*

This self flows with emotional cycles. It knows that presence does not require constancy ~ only honesty. It honors both the retreat and the return.

Symbols of the Day:

- A wave crashing, then pulling back, always becoming
- Moonstone, for emotional alignment and sacred feminine rhythm
- The High Priestess, inner knowing, seasonal wisdom, cyclical truth
- A sandbar only visible at low tide, treasure revealed through retreat

Reflection Prompts:

- Where do I judge myself for ebbing ~ and what might it feel like to allow that cycle?
- What part of me returns consistently, even when I forget it?
- How can I create space for my tides without labeling them "wrong"?

Integration Practice: Soul Tide Mapping

Draw two columns: "When I rise…" and "When I retreat…"
Under each, list how you feel, what helps, and what your soul is learning in those states.
Say:
"I am allowed to shift. My tides are not flaws ~ they are rhythms."
Then write:

- "The part of my tide I'm learning to honor is…"
- "Today, I flow with…"

Mantra for Today ~

"I rise and I recede. I am not broken. I am tidal ~ and I trust my rhythm."

August 28 – The Day of Healing Rain

A story of emotional nourishment, gentle renewal, and allowing the downpour to become your blessing

There once was a soul who avoided the storm.

Not because it feared getting wet ~ but because it didn't believe it had time to *feel*.

It stayed inside. Stayed productive. Stayed distant from the ache that hovered like a cloud.

But one day ~ as the Northern sky broke open with a sudden summer shower, or the Southern land softened beneath steady rain ~ the soul stopped running.

It stepped outside. Lifted its face. And let the rain come.

Not as punishment. As *presence*.

"You've held so much for so long," the water whispered, *"Let me hold you now."*

Tears mixed with rain. Not from despair ~ but from release.

The soul realized:

"This rain isn't undoing me. It's returning me."
To softness. To self. To soil ready for new growth.

Seasonal Awareness:

🌑 In the Northern Hemisphere, sudden emotional weather may rise. Let the "rain" fall ~ it is not breakdown, but breakthrough.

🌑 In the Southern Hemisphere, tender thaw is preparing the ground. Allow any tears or truths to soak in ~ they are watering what's to come.

Archetype of the Day: *The Rain-Receiver*

This self does not resist healing. It opens. It understands that some healing comes not from clarity ~ but from the *act of feeling*. It welcomes the storm when the soil is ready.

Symbols of the Day:

— A person standing still in rain, no umbrella, fully present
— Chalcedony, for emotional balance and gentle openness
— The Ace of Cups, new emotional beginnings, overflows of truth
— A windowpane streaked with rain, softening sharp views

Reflection Prompts:

- What healing am I resisting by staying "dry"?
- Where am I ready to let the emotional rain fall ~ even if I don't fully understand why?
- What might be softened by simply letting myself feel today?

Integration Practice: Rain-Welcome Ritual

If it's raining, step outside. If not, take a warm shower or place your hands under flowing water.

Say:

"I welcome the rain. I am not broken by feeling. I am nourished by what moves through me."

Then write:

- "What the rain reminds me of is…"
- "When I let myself feel, I…"

Mantra for Today ~

"I do not fear the rain. I receive it. I let it cleanse me ~ and make way for new life."

August 29 – The Day of Emotional Echo

A story of remembered feelings, subtle resonance, and honoring what returns to be felt more fully

There once was a soul who kept hearing things.

Not sounds. But feelings.

Old ones. Subtle echoes of past moments. Grief that had already been named. Joy that had already been lived.

And yet, there it was again ~ softly rising, asking to be felt once more.

The soul resisted at first:

"I've already worked through this."

But then one morning ~ as the Northern light touched familiar places in a new way, or the Southern air hinted at change with the scent of memory ~ the soul understood.

This wasn't repetition. It was resonance.

An emotional echo ~ not returning to haunt, but to *deepen*.

"This time," the soul whispered, *"I meet it differently."*

And so it did.

Not as a problem to solve. But as a reminder of what it had become ~ through everything it had felt before.

Seasonal Awareness:

🌑 In the Northern Hemisphere, end-of-season emotion may circle back. Let today be about meeting the feeling again ~ not to judge, but to recognize.

🌑 In the Southern Hemisphere, the echoes of winter may still linger. Allow yourself to listen ~ not as a delay, but as a necessary tuning.

Archetype of the Day: *The Resonant One*

This self hears beyond the surface. It receives the emotional returns ~ not as setbacks, but as sacred deepening. It honors echoes as signs of integration.

Symbols of the Day:

- A voice heard faintly in a canyon, not loud, but insistent
- Rose quartz, for heart reawakening and gentle reconnection
- The Six of Cups, emotional memory, past feelings renewed in new light

- A familiar object in a new setting, unchanged but transformed

Reflection Prompts:

- What feeling keeps returning to me ~ and how does it want to be met now?
- Where might I be mislabelling emotional resonance as regression?
- How has my response to this feeling changed?

Integration Practice: Echo Writing

Choose one feeling that has reappeared lately. Write a letter to it ~ as it was, and as it is now.

Say:

"You are not here to haunt me. You are here to remind me who I've become."

Then write:

- "What you're showing me today is…"
- "What I know now that I didn't know then is…"

Mantra for Today ~

"I meet this feeling again ~ not because I'm stuck, but because I'm ready to receive it with new eyes. Echoes are not regressions ~ they are reverberations of becoming."

August 30 – The Day of Deep Remembering

A story of soul memory, ancestral threads, and the quiet power of knowing you've carried this wisdom all along

There once was a soul who felt something stir ~ not in the body, not in the mind, but in a place deeper than both.

A truth resurfacing. A sensation of having been here before. Not as déjà vu ~ but as recognition.

The world hadn't changed. But the soul had stopped long enough to *remember*.

Then one evening ~ as the Northern dusk curled into rich violet tones, or the Southern morning shimmered through new buds ~ the soul felt it:

A pulse of old wisdom. A voice not quite its own. A knowing that rose from the roots, not the brain.

It wasn't a thought. It was *home*.

"You are not just learning," the inner voice whispered. *"You are remembering."*

The soul closed its eyes.

And in that sacred remembering ~ something within stood taller. Softer. Truer.

Seasonal Awareness:

🌑 In the Northern Hemisphere, the season edges toward reflection. Let today be about reconnecting with something older ~ and more inner.

🌑 In the Southern Hemisphere, as light returns, ancestral presence stirs too. Let remembrance walk beside renewal.

Archetype of the Day: *The Soul Rememberer*

This self carries wisdom through lifetimes ~ not as burden, but as sacred continuity. It does not seek novelty ~ it seeks resonance. It reclaims what's always been there.

Symbols of the Day:

— A spiral carved into stone, ancient and enduring
— Black moonstone, for ancestral connection and intuitive memory
— The Judgement card, soul-awakening, legacy, inner voice arising
— A song you don't remember learning ~ but know by heart

Reflection Prompts:

- What truth has resurfaced for me lately ~ not as new, but as familiar?
- Where do I feel guided by something older than myself?
- What wisdom might be ready to reawaken in me ~ if I stopped to listen?

Integration Practice: Soul Thread Meditation

Sit in stillness. Visualize a single thread of light connecting you to something timeless ~ a place, a voice, a presence.

Say:

"I remember now. I have carried this truth. I do not walk alone ~ I walk with what remembers."

Then write:

- *"The soul memory I reconnect with today is…"*
- *"This remembering strengthens me by…"*

Mantra for Today ~

"I do not always need to learn. Sometimes, I need to remember. My soul knows ~ and today, I listen."

August 31 – The Day of Sacred Closure

A story of ending with intention, integrating the unseen, and honoring the final page not as a finish, but as a foundation

There once was a soul who always rushed to the next chapter.

The last page of the book ~ skipped. The final breath of a season ~ overlooked. The goodbye ~ softened to avoid feeling it fully.

But one night ~ as the Northern stars gathered in quiet celebration, or the Southern earth exhaled in early bloom ~ the soul paused.

No distraction. No anticipation. Just this: the last day. And the first recognition of all it had become.

"This isn't just the end," the soul whispered. *"It's the becoming I couldn't yet see."*

The month hadn't changed the world ~ but it had changed the soul.

Every reflection. Every quiet awakening. Every moment of presence added something.

And now… something old could be released. And something deeper could begin.

Not because it was time to start over ~ but because it was time to *carry it forward*.

Seasonal Awareness:

🌑 In the Northern Hemisphere, a sacred pause settles in. Honor the full rhythm of this past season. Let closure be a slow, sacred exhale.

🌒 In the Southern Hemisphere, light is rising ~ but don't skip the final stillness. Completion allows newness to land on solid ground.

Archetype of the Day: *The Soul Closer*

This self knows how to stay through the final note. It doesn't rush. It completes with care, attention, and trust that endings are openings ~ turned inward.

Symbols of the Day:

- A book closed with a ribbon tucked inside, not forgotten, but honored
- Obsidian, for grounding, protection, and completion
- The World card, full-circle integration, wholeness
- A threshold lined with candles, one step beyond, but not yet taken

Reflection Prompts:

- What have I completed emotionally or spiritually this month ~ even if no one else noticed?
- What deserves a proper honoring before I move ahead?
- How can I mark this ending as sacred ~ not because it's dramatic, but because it's real?

Integration Practice: Sacred Closure Ritual

Light a candle or close your eyes in the dark.

Say aloud:

"I have lived this chapter. I have gathered its wisdom. I close it with reverence ~ and walk forward whole."

Then write:

- "The gift this month gave me was…"
- "What I leave behind ~ with love ~ is…"
- *"What I carry forward in truth is…"*

Mantra for Today ~

"I do not race to the next thing. I complete with care. This ending is my deep beginning ~ and I walk with all I've become."

August Reflection

'What Was Hidden, Now Flows'

A sacred reckoning.

You made it through the waters.

Not just the ones that felt graceful and luminous ~ but the ones that churned.

The still pools.

The emotional undertows.

The rising floods of memory and the tender trickles of clarity.

This month was never about the storm. It was about what the storm revealed.

You didn't just reflect ~ You remembered.

You didn't just shed ~ You softened.

You didn't just arrive ~ You *became*.

Journal Reflection: "How Have I Changed?"

Use these prompts to anchor your truth:

- What emotional response surprised me this month ~ and what did it show me?
- Where did I soften instead of control?
- What part of me did I finally meet in stillness, not judgment?
- What came full circle ~ not as closure, but as integration?

Then ask:

- What part of me feels clearer now, even without answers?
- What am I proud of that has no audience but me?

Soul Mirror ~ "The Symbols That Stayed With Me"

Recall a few images or metaphors from this month that resonated deeply:

- The whisper wind
- The inner storm
- The mirror of emotion
- The healing rain
- The soul tide

- The dimming light
- The echo returning home

What were they trying to say to you ~ softly, all along?

Gentle Continuation Practice

Choose one of the following to carry forward:

- Create a "Tidal Tracker" for next month ~ noting when you feel inward or outward each day
- Begin a Release Ritual Jar ~ small slips of paper for things you're ready to release emotionally
- Start a "What Returned Today?" journal ~ track feelings, dreams, symbols that reappear or repeat

The unknown didn't unravel you. It revealed you.
And what was once uncertain is now a current you can ride.

Closing Mantra for Volume 3 ~ *"I flowed through my depths. I let what needed to rise, rise. I am not lost in the unknown ~ I am luminous in it."*

September 1 – The Day of Carried Waters

A story of soul resilience, emotional memory, and learning to honor what you've held ~ without needing to hold it forever

There once was a soul who realized it had been carrying water for a very long time.

Not in buckets. But in body. In posture. In the quiet ache between breaths.

It had held space for others. Held silence for healing. Held sorrow it couldn't yet name.

But the soul never paused to ask:

"What am I still carrying ~ long after the well has run dry?"

One early morning ~ as the Northern winds whispered across calm lakes, or the Southern clouds broke gently into pale blue promise ~ the soul stopped.

It knelt beside a stream. Watched it run. Watched it *move*.

Not because it had to. But because it could.

"This is what I've forgotten," the soul whispered. *"Water is meant to be carried ~ but also poured."*

And so, the soul let the weight of all it had held trickle down its spine, out through the soles of its feet, and back into the earth.

Not lost ~ but *returned*.

Seasonal Awareness:

🌘 In the Northern Hemisphere, the air begins to shift. It is time to ask: What weight are you ready to set down ~ not with anger, but with reverence?

🌑 In the Southern Hemisphere, growth stirs. Clear the vessel. What you make room for now will shape what flows into you next.

Archetype of the Day: *The Water Bearer*

This self does not resist the weight. But neither does it cling to what was only meant to be temporary. It learns to hold ~ and then *release*. It trusts that flow is sacred when it circles back.

Symbols of the Day:

— A clay jug tipped gently over a garden, nourishing, not draining

— Aquamarine, for emotional clarity and heart flow

- The Temperance card, balancing what is kept and what is shared
- A river stone smoothed over time, heavy, yes ~ but shaped by surrender

Reflection Prompts:

- What have I been carrying emotionally, energetically, or relationally ~ for far longer than I needed to?
- Where am I still holding what I once needed ~ but no longer do?
- What would it feel like to pour this water back ~ as a gift, not a burden?

Integration Practice: Pouring Ritual

Fill a bowl or cup with water. Hold it in both hands. Name what you've been carrying aloud or silently.

Then pour it slowly into the earth, a plant, or a sink.

Say:

"I honor what I've carried. And now, I release it ~ not in rejection, but in return."

Write:

- "Today I poured out…"
- "Now I make space for…"

Mantra for Today ~

"I do not carry what is no longer mine. I release what was sacred ~ and trust that emptiness can hold just as much as fullness."

September 2 – The Day of Echoed Wisdom

A story of repetition with meaning, soul evolution, and recognizing when something returns not to test you, but to prove how much you've grown

There once was a soul who found itself back in a familiar situation.

The words felt the same. The discomfort, familiar. The emotional terrain ~ almost identical to what it had faced before.

And at first, the soul felt defeated.

"Why is this happening again?" it asked.

But then, something shifted.

This time, the soul responded differently. Softer. Clearer. Wiser.

And that's when it understood:

"This isn't a failure. This is a return ~ with more truth."

Not everything that circles back is a mistake. Sometimes, it's an *echo* ~ calling you to notice your own evolution.

The situation hadn't changed. But the soul had.

Seasonal Awareness:

🌑 In the Northern Hemisphere, seasonal reflection deepens. You may notice old themes reappear ~ but meet them as *proof* of who you've become.

🌒 In the Southern Hemisphere, renewal comes with repetition. Let recurring patterns show you what you've already grown beyond ~ and what wisdom now lives in your bones.

Archetype of the Day: *The Echo Listener*

This self hears what is familiar ~ but listens with new ears. It sees old lessons not as failures, but as mirrors of maturity. It honors growth not through avoidance, but through response.

Symbols of the Day:

— A voice spoken into a canyon, returning not as repetition ~ but resonance
— Iolite, for perspective, soul clarity, and deep intuition
— The Wheel of Fortune, cycles, karmic movement, returning with insight
— A spiral staircase, rising while circling ~ never quite the same step twice

Reflection Prompts:

- What situation or emotion has reappeared lately ~ and how am I responding differently this time?
- Where can I give myself credit for growth, even if the external looks familiar?
- What wisdom has echoed back ~ not to challenge me, but to confirm me?

Integration Practice: Echo Recognition

Draw a small spiral. At the center, write a phrase or situation that has returned. On each curve outward, write one way you've grown or shifted since the first time it occurred.

Say:

"This is not a loop. This is a spiral. I am not repeating ~ I am rising."

Then write:

- *"What's different about me now is…"*
- *"How I choose to walk this echo today is…"*

Mantra for Today ~

"I am not where I started. I honor what returns, because it reflects my growth. I rise through the echo ~ and carry new truth forward."

September 3 – The Day of Soft Power

A story of quiet strength, calm assertion, and learning that gentleness is not weakness, but wisdom in motion

There once was a soul who thought it had to be loud to be heard.

It tried to speak in certainty. To lead with force. To be undeniable ~ even when its truth was small and sacred.

But this only made it tired.

Then one clear morning ~ as the Northern wind moved the trees without snapping a single branch, or the Southern light stretched low and wide over dew-kissed earth ~ the soul witnessed something quiet:

A child offering comfort without words. A breeze shifting the entire mood of a room. A stone holding heat long after the fire had gone.

"This," the soul realized, *"is power ~ not for display, but for depth."*

And in that moment, it let go of the need to prove.

It chose instead to be steady. Present. Kind ~ and clear. And it changed the entire energy of the space around it.

Not because it took over.

But because it *settled in*.

Seasonal Awareness:

🌑 In the Northern Hemisphere, this is a time when your presence may carry more weight than your performance. Let your impact be felt in tone, not volume.

🌑 In the Southern Hemisphere, early growth requires protection ~ not through defense, but through grace. Let your strength be rooted in steadiness.

Archetype of the Day: *The Steady Flame*

This self is calm, but not passive. It chooses its influence not with pressure, but with clarity. It leads by example ~ not explosion.

It is powerful, *and soft*, at the same time.

- **Symbols of the Day:**
- A single candle in a dark room, gentle, unwavering
- Amazonite, for harmony, compassionate boundaries, and voice
- The Strength card, emotional resilience, inner grace, truth without aggression
- A stream that carves stone over time, patient and persistent

Reflection Prompts:

- Where have I been told I need to be louder, firmer, or more aggressive to be powerful?
- What does soft power look like in my life ~ and how can I embody it with integrity?
- What part of me is strongest when I am quietest?

Integration Practice: Silent Strength

Take five minutes today to simply be present ~ in a conversation, in a room, in a moment ~ without needing to explain, defend, or impress.

Say:

"My presence speaks. My softness leads. I do not need to raise my voice to raise my energy."

Then write:

- *"Where my soft power showed up today…"*
- *"What changed because I didn't push ~ I stayed."*

Mantra for Today ~

"I am soft ~ and strong. I influence through peace, not pressure. My strength is not loud ~ it is lived."

September 4 – The Day of Emotional Refuge

A story of safety within, sacred shelter, and learning to be your own sanctuary when the world feels too loud

There once was a soul who kept searching for a place to land.

It wandered through conversations, distractions, even relationships ~ looking for somewhere to rest. Somewhere to be soft. Somewhere to stop performing and simply *exist*.

But nowhere felt quite right.

Until one evening ~ as the Northern sky dulled into twilight hush, or the Southern birds quieted into early dusk ~ the soul turned inward.

And asked,

"What if I stopped looking for refuge ~ and started becoming it?"

It sat still. Breathed deeply. And for the first time, created space within itself:

No judgment. No fixing. Just permission to feel, without performance.

And in that stillness, the soul realized ~

It had always been allowed to be its own home.

Not a fortress. A refuge.

Soft walls. Gentle light. A place where every part of itself could *arrive*.

Seasonal Awareness:

🌒 In the Northern Hemisphere, as the season cools, emotional needs shift. Give yourself space today ~ to step back, to be held, to not explain.

🌘 In the Southern Hemisphere, life may ask for energy again. Let your energy rise only from safety ~ not obligation. Let your soul choose when to emerge.

Archetype of the Day: *The Inner Sanctuary*

This self is not hard. It is *held*. It offers a place inside where no part of you is rejected.

It becomes refuge ~ not just for itself, but eventually, for others.

Symbols of the Day:

— A tent glowing with soft light in the forest, small, safe, sacred

- Moonstone, for inner reflection, emotional safety, and feminine healing
- The Four of Swords, rest, retreat, sacred pause
- A warm hand placed over the heart, wordless, steady

Reflection Prompts:

- What part of me most needs a safe space today ~ and have I made room for it?
- Where have I been seeking refuge externally, when my inner self is asking for my presence instead?
- How would I treat myself if I were the one I was trying to protect?

Integration Practice: Create Your Refuge

Find or create a small space today that feels safe ~ a corner, a chair, a room, even just your breath.

Say:

"I am safe in myself. I am welcome here. I am not too much ~ I am already home."

Then write:

- "My refuge today felt like…"
- *"What changed when I allowed myself to land was…"*

Mantra for Today ~

"I do not need to search to be held. I offer myself safety ~ by showing up without fear. I am a sanctuary ~ for my whole self."

September 5 – The Day of Honest Openings

A story of truth gently revealed, vulnerability without force, and learning that openness is a practice, not a performance

There once was a soul who kept its truths tightly sealed.

Not because it wanted to hide ~ but because it had once been open, and that openness had been misunderstood.

So it closed. Softly. Quietly. Without bitterness ~ but with caution.

And still, it longed ~ for connection, for ease, for the freedom to speak its heart.

Then one late morning ~ as the Northern air turned crisp with the scent of turning leaves, or the Southern petals stretched open to the warming sun ~ the soul sat near a window.

It opened it just a crack. Let in the air. Let out a breath.

"I don't have to fling open the doors," it whispered. *"I can open one part of me ~ one truth ~ and let that be enough today."*

And it was.

No breakdown. No breakthrough.

Just *presence* ~ held in the quiet honesty of being seen, one layer at a time.

Seasonal Awareness:

🌑 In the Northern Hemisphere, you may feel the instinct to pull in. Let today be a moment of safe opening ~ not for others, but for yourself.

🌒 In the Southern Hemisphere, spring energy rises. Instead of bursting forward, choose one authentic reveal. Let your truth emerge like a petal ~ not a performance.

Archetype of the Day: *The Honest Opener*

This self does not perform vulnerability. It offers what is real ~ not all at once, but in rhythm with the heart.

It opens not to be approved of ~ but to be *true*.

Symbols of the Day:

— A window cracked open in a quiet room, fresh air moving gently through

— Blue lace agate, for clear expression and gentle self-disclosure

- The Page of Swords, youthful truth, honest curiosity, brave beginnings
- A letter left on a table, not urgent, but full of truth

Reflection Prompts:

- What truth in me is ready to be shared ~ even if only with myself?
- Where have I been closed ~ not out of fear, but out of old protection?
- What would one small, honest opening look like today?

Integration Practice: Truth Crack Ritual

Write a sentence ~ just one ~ that feels honest and slightly vulnerable. Say it out loud to yourself. Then whisper:

"That was real. That was enough."

Optionally, share it with someone you trust. If not, simply witness yourself.

Then write:

- *"The truth I cracked open today was…"*
- *"What softened in me after I spoke it was…"*

Mantra for Today ~

"I open in rhythm with my readiness. My honesty is not for approval ~ it is for alignment. I am safe to open ~ one truth at a time."

September 6 – The Day of Soft Illumination

A story of gentle light, unseen wisdom, and discovering that the glow you need doesn't have to blind ~ only guide

There once was a soul who thought it had to shine brightly to be worthy.

It tried to be radiant ~ always. Always wise. Always certain. Always clear. But it felt exhausted.

Then one hushed evening ~ as the Northern sun fell quietly beneath early autumn clouds, or the Southern moon rose into the growing breath of spring ~ the soul lit a single candle.

Not for others to see. Just for itself.

And in that flickering glow, it found something more valuable than brightness:

Soft truth. Quiet warmth. The kind of light that didn't expose ~ but comforted.

The soul realized that sometimes the brightest wisdom is also the gentlest. Not all knowing arrives with clarity. Some arrives with *care*. And it is enough.

Seasonal Awareness:

🌕 In the Northern Hemisphere, the outward light dims. Let your guidance come from within ~ not as pressure, but as peaceful knowing.

🌑 In the Southern Hemisphere, awakening light may feel too harsh. Today is for choosing *soft clarity* ~ the kind that nourishes, not overwhelms.

Archetype of the Day: *The Gentle Guide*

This self does not lead with volume. It walks with light cupped in its palms ~ steady, quiet, safe.

It doesn't need all the answers. It only needs to stay with what's real, in this moment.

Symbols of the Day:

- A candle in a window at dusk, small but unwavering
- Selenite, for divine clarity, peaceful truth, and crown wisdom
- The Star card, hope in shadow, soft insight, soul renewal

— A night lamp turned on during a storm, not bright ~ but enough

Reflection Prompts:

— What kind of light am I seeking today ~ harsh truth, or gentle clarity?
— Where in my life could soft illumination guide me better than intensity?
— What truth glows inside me that doesn't need to be loud to be valid?

Integration Practice: Candle Reflection

Light a candle (or imagine one if unavailable). Sit in its glow and ask:

"What do I need to know right now ~ not perfectly, but kindly?"

— Breathe. Listen. Then write:
— "The soft wisdom rising in me is…"
— "*I will follow it gently by…*" Let your guidance be kind.

Mantra for Today ~

"I do not need to blaze to belong. I shine softly ~ and that is enough. My truth glows ~ steady and sacred."

September 7 – The Day of Deep Listening

A story of quiet attunement, hearing what isn't said, and honoring the sacred wisdom that speaks through silence

There once was a soul who spent a lifetime speaking ~ trying to say it right, be heard, be understood.

But in all that speaking, something got lost.

One morning ~ as the Northern leaves rustled in windless air, or the Southern branches creaked in early morning warmth ~ the soul sat down and simply listened.

At first, all it noticed was noise. Distraction. Surface-level static.

Then something deeper emerged. The rhythm of breath. The tremble beneath a heartbeat. The voice beneath the story.

"There is wisdom here," the soul realized, *"that words have never touched."*

It listened without fixing. Heard without needing to reply.

And in that stillness, it received something rare:

A truth that *couldn't be spoken*, but that changed everything.

Seasonal Awareness:

🌘 In the Northern Hemisphere, the world begins to quiet. Let today be about attunement ~ not through action, but through listening.

🌒 In the Southern Hemisphere, as new sound returns, don't miss the subtle voices rising. Listen with more than your ears ~ listen with your presence.

Archetype of the Day: *The Soul Listener*

This self does not interrupt. It doesn't prepare a response while others speak. It simply *receives* ~ fully, kindly, and with reverence for what's unsaid.

Symbols of the Day:

- A shell held to the ear, revealing an ocean that's nowhere nearby
- Lapis lazuli, for inner hearing, communication, and truth alignment
- The High Priestess, sacred knowing, wordless insight, intuition awakened
- A pause in conversation, where everything real finally rises

Reflection Prompts:

— What am I not hearing ~ from myself, from others, or from the world ~ because I've been too quick to speak or decide?
— Where is silence trying to show me something I've overlooked?
— What does it feel like to be truly heard ~ and how can I offer that today?

Integration Practice: 3-Minute Listening Ritual

Set a timer. Sit in silence. Let every sound ~ internal and external ~ rise without reaction.

Say:

"I am listening ~ not to judge, not to fix, but to receive."

Then write:

— "What I heard in the quiet was…"
— *"What softened or opened in me through listening…"*

Let silence be your teacher.

Mantra for Today ~

"I listen with my whole being. I receive what is real ~ even when it has no words. In deep listening ~ I return to truth."

September 8 – The Day of the Unspoken Yes

A story of soul agreement, embodied truth, and honoring the moments where alignment speaks louder than words

There once was a soul who had said yes too often ~ out of politeness, guilt, or fear of being left behind.

But none of those yeses felt alive. They were performances ~ not permissions.

Then one quiet afternoon ~ as the Northern sun tilted lower on the horizon, or the Southern breeze carried the scent of new leaves ~ the soul felt something different:

A warmth in the chest. A softening behind the eyes. A gentle pull, deeper than logic, quieter than speech.

It didn't ask for approval. It didn't come with pressure.

It simply whispered:

"Yes."

Not to someone else. To *life*. To alignment. To the part of self that finally felt fully ready.

No justification. No announcement.

Just a knowing.

"This yes is mine. I don't have to say it ~ I only need to feel it."

Seasonal Awareness:

🌑 In the Northern Hemisphere, this is a time of refining what's worth your energy. Let today's yes come from depth ~ not demand.

🌒 In the Southern Hemisphere, new opportunities may call. Say yes not out of obligation, but out of embodied resonance.

Archetype of the Day: *The Inner Aligned One*

This self doesn't respond from reflex ~ it responds from reverence. It recognizes the difference between pressure and permission. It says yes not because it "should" ~ but because it *is ready*.

Symbols of the Day:

— A body leaning slightly forward, without hesitation ~ just trust

— Sunstone, for joyful affirmation, soul consent, and personal power

- The Two of Wands, conscious choice, inner agreement, ready movement
- A door already opening before a knock, not rushed, but timed by alignment

Reflection Prompts:

- Where have I said yes out of fear or habit?
- What is asking for my true yes ~ even if I never say it out loud?
- How do I know when a yes is coming from alignment ~ not from urgency?

Integration Practice: Felt Yes Scan

Close your eyes. Breathe into your belly and chest. Recall a recent "yes" and ask: *Did my body agree?*

Now, think of one thing today you want to say yes to ~ silently, sacredly.

Say:

"I honor the yes that rises from within. I say yes without performance ~ only with presence."

Then write:

- "Today I say yes to…"
- "Because I feel it in…" *(name the part of your body or emotion)*

Mantra for Today ~

"My yes does not need applause. It needs honesty. I say yes where I am whole ~ and where my soul leads."

September 9 – The Day of Gentle Completion

A story of soft endings, circular grace, and learning to close without collapsing

There once was a soul who believed that endings had to be dramatic.

That closure meant goodbye. That finishing meant failure or finality.

So it resisted completing things. Let projects trail. Let relationships fray. Let self-reflection stay one page from finished.

But one golden dusk ~ as the Northern fields quieted into harvested stillness, or the Southern air warmed with a hopeful hush ~ the soul completed something small:

A note. A thought. A soft breath.

And it realized:

"I don't have to collapse to be complete. I can end gently ~ and carry what matters forward."

The ending didn't hurt. It healed.

Not because it erased what had been, but because it honored it ~ and made space for what might be.

Seasonal Awareness:

🌑 In the Northern Hemisphere, harvesting energy asks you to acknowledge what's been completed ~ not with finality, but with care.

🌑 In the Southern Hemisphere, early stirrings may tempt you to skip the final pause. Today reminds you: a gentle ending builds a stronger beginning.

Archetype of the Day: *The Graceful Closer*

This self doesn't dramatize or delay. It brings care to the final step. It knows that closure is not absence ~ it is *integration*.

It closes the circle ~ and blesses the next.

Symbols of the Day:

— A knot being tied at the end of a thread, not to bind ~ but to secure
— Chrysoprase, for acceptance, closure, and emotional serenity
— The World card, full-circle truth, whole-soul knowing, release with purpose
— A candle gently blown out, with gratitude in the breath

Reflection Prompts:

- What in my life is ready to be completed ~ gently, not dramatically?
- Where am I holding on because I fear what completion might mean?

What wisdom wants to come through this ending ~ if I choose to honor it?

Integration Practice: Graceful Goodbye

Choose one thing to complete today: a journal entry, a task, an emotion, a habit.

As you close it, place a hand over your heart.

Say:

"I do not lose what I complete. I gather it into who I am. This circle is whole ~ and I thank it."

Then write:

- *"Today I gently completed…"*
- *"What I carry forward from it is…"*

Mantra for Today ~

"I do not rush to finish. I do not avoid the end. I complete with grace ~ and walk forward whole."

September 10 – The Day of Soul Transparency

A story of clarity without shame, inner truth revealed, and learning that you don't have to be exposed to be seen

There once was a soul who wore layers.

Not clothes ~ but masks. Smiles that hid sorrow. Certainty that cloaked doubt. Silence that protected truth.

The soul had learned ~ long ago ~ that being "real" came at a cost. So it stayed covered. Polished. Protected.

But one day ~ as the Northern skies cleared into lucid blue, or the Southern air shimmered softly with golden light ~ the soul stood near a window and saw itself in the glass.

Not distorted. Not hidden. Just *there*.

And for the first time, it didn't flinch.

"This is me," it whispered. *"Not polished. Not prepared. Just present."*

It didn't throw the masks away.

It simply stopped *leading* with them.

Because real transparency isn't about being fully seen by others ~ it's about no longer hiding from yourself.

Seasonal Awareness:

🌑 In the Northern Hemisphere, clarity grows as the light softens. Today, choose truth ~ not as confession, but as alignment.

🌑 In the Southern Hemisphere, with new energy returning, resist the pressure to perform. Let your soul be visible, even in its gentlest form.

Archetype of the Day: *The Clear One*

This self isn't raw ~ it's *real*. It doesn't seek to shock or impress. It stands in its truth with softness and sovereignty.

It doesn't expose. It *reveals*.

Symbols of the Day:

- A pane of clean glass, separating nothing ~ only holding light
- Clear quartz, for inner clarity, energy alignment, and soul truth
- The Queen of Swords, honesty, discernment, loving precision

- A pool of still water, reflecting everything without distortion

Reflection Prompts:

- What part of me am I still hiding ~ not to protect it, but out of old habit?
- Where could more soul transparency lead to deeper peace, not just visibility?
- What does it feel like to be honest ~ not loud, but whole?

Integration Practice: Mirror Moment

Stand in front of a mirror. Look into your own eyes.

Say:

"I see you. I honor what's real. I no longer hide what I've already healed."

Then write:

- "The truth I no longer need to cover is..."
- *"When I see myself clearly, I..."*

Mantra for Today ~

"I am not exposed. I am revealed. My soul is clear ~ and I am safe to be seen."

September 11 – The Day of Devotional Presence

A story of sacred attention, holy now-ness, and remembering that being fully with what is ~ is the deepest form of love

There once was a soul who longed for meaning.

It searched through teachings. Gathered mantras. Stacked moments like steps to enlightenment.

But still, something felt distant.

Then one quiet morning ~ as the Northern light filtered through unmoving trees, or the Southern breeze stirred a single curtain in the sun ~ the soul paused.

Not to study. Not to plan. Not to "do."

It simply sat. Breathed. Listened.

And in that still presence, something sacred entered.

Not as a sign. Not as a breakthrough. But as a *being-with*.

"This moment is enough," the soul whispered. *"And when I stay with it fully ~ so am I."*

It had found devotion. Not as religion. But as reverence.

Reverence for now. Reverence for self. Reverence for the way presence itself could become a prayer.

Seasonal Awareness:

🌕 In the Northern Hemisphere, the season invites you into inner devotion. Let today be about how deeply you can *be* ~ without needing to become.

🌑 In the Southern Hemisphere, emerging energy can feel scattered. Anchor it not with force, but with *presence*. What you give your attention to, you bless.

Archetype of the Day: *The Devoted One*

This self is not urgent. It is anchored.

It offers full presence ~ not because it fixes anything, but because presence *itself* is holy.

Symbols of the Day:

- A cup placed slowly on a table, not rushed, fully witnessed
- Amethyst, for grounded presence and spiritual stillness

- The Hierophant card, sacred discipline, embodied teaching, ritual in the now
- A pair of eyes meeting with no agenda, just presence

Reflection Prompts:

- Where am I rushing past the sacred in search of something else?
- What would happen if I met today with complete, unhurried presence?
- What becomes holy when I fully show up to it ~ even for a few breaths?

Integration Practice: Micro Devotion

Choose one small act today ~ making tea, folding clothes, lighting a candle ~ and do it slowly, prayerfully.

Say:

"This is not a task. This is a temple. My attention makes it sacred."

Then write:

- "The moment I met fully today was…"
- *"And in that meeting, I found…"*

¶
¶
¶
¶
¶
¶
¶
¶
¶
¶
¶
¶

Mantra for Today ~

"I do not need to perform the sacred. I only need to be with it. My presence is my devotion ~ and I am here."

September 12 – The Day of Soul-Tethering

A story of inner anchoring, sacred commitment, and remembering the quiet strength of choosing what holds you steady

There once was a soul who drifted beautifully.

It explored. Wandered. Loved widely and sought freely.

But in all that movement, it began to lose something:

Its center.

It didn't feel lost, exactly ~ but unmoored. As if it belonged to everything... and nothing at all.

Then one still afternoon ~ as the Northern trees stood anchored in golden quiet, or the Southern roots stretched quietly beneath early bloom ~ the soul knelt down and touched the ground.

"What holds me?" it asked. *"What do I return to, when I've forgotten myself?"*

And it saw it ~

Not a rule. Not a person. But a practice. A promise. A truth it had whispered to itself long ago, and nearly forgotten.

That was its tether. Not to bind it ~ but to *hold* it.

And the soul, for the first time in a long time, felt still ~ and safe.

Seasonal Awareness:

🌑 In the Northern Hemisphere, movement begins to slow. Let this be a day to re-anchor ~ not in what is loud, but in what is lasting.

🌑 In the Southern Hemisphere, new growth is exciting ~ but needs grounding. Let your roots go down before you rise up.

Archetype of the Day: *The Anchored One*

This self chooses what holds it. Not out of fear ~ but out of alignment. It tethers itself to meaning, practice, truth ~ and lets that still point guide the movement.

Symbols of the Day:

— A stone tied with a thread, small but grounded
— Hematite, for grounding, clarity, and spiritual alignment
— The Four of Wands, soul commitment, sacred returning, chosen belonging
— A tree leaning in the wind, but never uprooted, held in place by deep roots

Reflection Prompts:

— What keeps me steady ~ especially when everything else changes?
— What promise or practice have I made to myself that I've drifted from ~ and want to return to?
— Where do I need less motion ~ and more meaning?

Integration Practice: Tethering Statement

Write one sentence that holds your soul steady ~ a value, belief, or promise.

Then say:

"This is my tether. I return here. I am not lost ~ I am aligned."

Then write:

— *"My tether today is…"*
— *"I will stay connected by…"*

Let it guide you back.

Mantra for Today ~

"I do not resist movement ~ but I stay rooted. I choose what holds me. I return to truth ~ and remember who I am."

September 13 – The Day of the Unfolding Self

A story of becoming slowly, trusting the process, and learning that identity isn't fixed ~ it's revealed over time

There once was a soul who thought it had to be defined.

It tried on titles. Chased clarity. Carved out certainty in stone.

But each time it thought, *"This is who I am,"* life gently peeled back another layer. Not to confuse ~ but to *deepen*.

One morning ~ as the Northern fog rose from the ground in slow spirals, or the Southern petals loosened under the warmth of spring light ~ the soul stopped asking, *"Who am I?"*

And instead whispered:

"Who am I becoming ~ right now?"

It didn't try to finish the sentence. It didn't force an answer. It just *unfolded*.

Softly. In rhythm. In trust.

And it realized ~ identity isn't a definition. It's a movement. A spiral. A bloom that never ends.

Seasonal Awareness:

🌑 In the Northern Hemisphere, this is a time to witness subtle shifts. Allow who you are to emerge without needing to name it yet.

🌑 In the Southern Hemisphere, new energy rises. Let your identity expand gently ~ not as reinvention, but as re-revealing.

Archetype of the Day: *The Becoming One*

This self does not cling to labels. It trusts process over polish. It knows that the soul reveals itself layer by layer ~ not to confuse, but to invite presence.

Symbols of the Day:

- A fern unfurling, slow, natural, deliberate
- Malachite, for transformation, identity healing, and heart alignment
- The Death card, symbolic endings that lead to true emergence
- A hand reaching toward light, unsure of the shape, but sure of the pull

Reflection Prompts:

- Where have I been trying to define myself too tightly ~ and what part of me is still unfolding?
- What identity do I need to release ~ not because it was wrong, but because I've outgrown it?
- What would it feel like to let myself emerge ~ instead of arrive?

Integration Practice: Self-Unfolding Ritual

Write 3 versions of the sentence: "Right now, I am someone who is becoming…"

Let them be incomplete. Let them breathe.

Then say:

"I allow myself to evolve. I do not rush clarity. I unfold in my own rhythm ~ and that is sacred."

Then write:

- "Today, I noticed myself becoming…"
- "This version of me feels…"

Mantra for Today ~

"I am not fixed. I am unfolding. I am the becoming ~ and that is enough."

September 14 – The Day of Inner Lightness

A story of releasing the unseen weight, remembering joy, and discovering that freedom often begins from within

There once was a soul who didn't realize how heavy it had become.

It wasn't carrying tragedy. It wasn't drowning in sorrow.

But it had accumulated small weights ~ unspoken obligations, old tensions, forgotten self-promises, tiny expectations.

They hung around its shoulders like invisible cloaks.

Then one afternoon ~ as the Northern wind skipped through fading fields, or the Southern air danced lightly between blooms ~ the soul laughed.

Not at anything profound. Just a moment. A small, bright flicker of presence.

And in that laugh, something lifted.

"I forgot I was carrying that," the soul said.

It hadn't needed a breakthrough. It needed a breath.

A moment to remember that lightness isn't the absence of depth ~ it's the presence of permission.

Permission to release. To rise. To be whole ~ and weightless, too.

Seasonal Awareness:

🌗 In the Northern Hemisphere, the inner and outer world invite a letting-go. Lightness today may not look dramatic ~ but it will feel like truth.

🌘 In the Southern Hemisphere, as new growth calls, release what would make joy feel like work. Let ease be the soil from which your joy emerges.

Archetype of the Day: *The Light Bearer*

This self doesn't ignore pain ~ it breathes through it. It doesn't bypass truth ~ it travels light. It knows that shedding isn't denial ~ it's devotion to life.

Symbols of the Day:

— A feather lifted by breeze, no resistance, pure presence

— Citrine, for lightness, clarity, and joy-infused energy

— The Fool card, trust, freedom, walking with wonder

- A bundle being unwrapped and scattered to the wind, not discarded ~ released

Reflection Prompts:

- What am I carrying that no longer belongs to me ~ not because it's bad, but because it's finished?
- Where could I choose ease today ~ not as escape, but as alignment?
- Allow yourself to be free of just one thing, quietly?

Integration Practice: Release Breath

Take three long exhales.

With each, imagine letting go of something small but lingering.

Say:

"I do not need to carry what I've outgrown. I make space for lightness. I am allowed to feel ease."

Then write:

- *"What I released today was…"*
- *"The space it created inside me feels like…"*

Mantra for Today ~

"Lightness is not emptiness. It is sacred release. I breathe out what I no longer need ~ and rise."

September 15 – The Day of Sacred Discernment

A story of quiet clarity, inner knowing, and choosing not by pressure ~ but by presence

There once was a soul who confused movement with progress.

It said yes to everything that sounded good. Every invitation. Every spark. Every voice that whispered, *"You should."*

But with each yes, it felt less like itself.

Then one clear morning ~ as the Northern skies offered sharp contrast between shadow and light, or the Southern ground stirred with decision-making energy ~ the soul stood still.

It closed its eyes. Placed one hand over its chest. And asked:

"Does this nourish me ~ or deplete me?"

The question rang like a tuning fork. And with it came a knowing ~ simple, sharp, and serene.

That was discernment. Not a rule. Not a fear. A remembering.

The soul didn't need to justify, explain, or defend.

It simply chose. From alignment. With love.

And that choice felt like freedom.

Seasonal Awareness:

🌑 In the Northern Hemisphere, clarity deepens. Let the shift of season guide you into inner decision-making ~ not reaction, but resonance.

🌑 In the Southern Hemisphere, new paths emerge. Pause before choosing. Let discernment, not urgency, move you forward.

Archetype of the Day: *The Aligned Chooser*

This self trusts its inner compass. It doesn't chase ~ it calibrates. It discerns not from fear, but from quiet devotion to what is truly alive inside.

Symbols of the Day:

— A fork in a forest path, one route softly glowing
— Sodalite, for inner truth, logic + intuition, and wise decision-making
— The Justice card, clarity, balance, aligned action
— A scale with a single feather and a single stone, both true ~ but different

Reflection Prompts:

- Where have I been saying yes or no from fear ~ not from fullness?
- What is asking for a decision ~ and how do I want to feel in that choice?
- What would it look like to choose with calm, not performance?

Integration Practice: Inner Compass Check

Take a current decision or opportunity. Write down both options.

Place one hand on your heart. Breathe.

Say:

"I choose from within. I listen beneath the noise. I trust my truth."

Then write:

- "Today, I choose to..."
- *"Because it feels like..."* (describe the physical/emotional feeling)

Mantra for Today ~

"I do not react ~ I respond. I do not chase ~ I choose. I move in sacred clarity ~ and stay with my truth."

September 16 – The Day of Soft Boundaries

A story of protection without walls, self-honoring without hardness, and learning that saying no can be an act of sacred care

There once was a soul who didn't know where it ended and others began.

It wanted to be kind. To be open. To be trusted.

So it said yes ~ often. Held space ~ endlessly. Gave energy ~ without pause.

Until the edges blurred. Until it no longer knew what *it* wanted.

Then one quiet morning ~ as the Northern mist lingered like a veil on the fields, or the Southern sun warmed only the space it touched ~ the soul stepped outside and drew a circle in the dirt.

Not to shut others out. But to remind itself where it began.

It whispered:

"This is my yes. This is my no. This is where I can love you ~ without losing me."

And suddenly, the soul felt strong.

Not sharp. Not defensive.

Just clear. Just whole.

Because boundaries were not walls. They were *wisdom*.

Seasonal Awareness:

🌑 In the Northern Hemisphere, personal energy wanes with the season. Protect what remains. Let soft boundaries preserve your inner light.

🌑 In the Southern Hemisphere, growth begins. Let boundaries shape the direction of that growth ~ so you expand with intention, not exhaustion.

Archetype of the Day: *The Soul Protector*

This self does not push back ~ it simply holds steady. It knows where it ends and others begin. It does not perform generosity. It offers presence from a place that is *resourced*.

Symbols of the Day:

— A garden with a low wooden fence, visible, gentle, respected

— Black tourmaline, for grounding, energetic protection, and calm presence

- The Nine of Wands, resilient boundaries, lessons earned, self-trust
- A circle drawn in sand, not to trap ~ but to hold

Reflection Prompts:

- Where am I giving more than I can sustain ~ and what boundary would protect my peace?
- What is one boundary I've been afraid to hold ~ and what fear is beneath that?
- How can I love others better by loving myself through clearer space?

Integration Practice: Boundary Visualization

Close your eyes and imagine a soft circle of light around you. Say:

"This is my sacred space. I choose what enters. I choose what stays. I choose me ~ with love."

Then write:

- "One boundary I will honor today is…"
- *"Holding this boundary helps me…"*

Mantra for Today ~

"My boundaries are not walls ~ they are bridges back to myself. I protect what is sacred ~ not out of fear, but out of care. I stay whole ~ and love from there."

September 17 – The Day of Gentle Truth-Telling

A story of speaking from the heart, honoring truth with compassion, and remembering that softness doesn't silence truth ~ it delivers it with grace

There once was a soul who silenced itself to keep the peace.

It bit its tongue. Smiled politely. Withheld honesty in favor of harmony.

But inside, something frayed. A quiet ache. The feeling of being unheard ~ even by itself.

Then one twilight ~ as the Northern winds rustled trees like whispered reminders, or the Southern air settled into early-evening light ~ the soul spoke.

Not loudly. Not sharply.

But clearly.

"This is my truth. I'm not saying it to hurt you ~ I'm saying it to honor me."

And the air changed.

Not with drama. But with dignity.

The soul had not attacked. It had revealed.

And in doing so, it remembered:

Truth doesn't need to roar. It only needs to *arrive* ~ wrapped in care, but firm in presence.

Seasonal Awareness:

🌑 In the Northern Hemisphere, expression grows inward. Let today's truth be small, steady, and rooted in self-respect.

🌑 In the Southern Hemisphere, clarity returns. Use it not to confront, but to *connect* ~ by speaking from truth, not tension.

Archetype of the Day: *The Soul Speaker*

This self chooses truth ~ not as weapon, but as offering. It knows that honesty can coexist with love. It doesn't speak to win ~ it speaks to be *real*.

Symbols of the Day:

- A note slipped under a door, quiet, considered, true
- Blue kyanite, for clear communication, emotional balance, and truth-telling

- The Ace of Swords, new clarity, aligned speech, cutting through fog
- A hand held while speaking difficult words, connection without compromise

Reflection Prompts:

- What truth have I been holding ~ not because it's wrong to speak, but because I fear how it will land?
- How can I say what's real ~ with softness, not silence?
- What changes in me when I hear my own voice speak truth clearly?

Integration Practice: Speak the Small Truth

Name one thing today ~ aloud ~ that is true for you. It doesn't have to be big. Just honest.

Say:

"This is real for me. I speak it with care. My voice is not a threat ~ it is a bridge."

Then write:

- "The truth I spoke today was…"
- *"And when I heard myself say it, I felt…"*

Mantra for Today ~

"I speak with clarity, not cruelty. I reveal, not to control ~ but to connect. My truth is sacred ~ and I am safe to share it."

September 18 – The Day of Inner Harmony

A story of soul alignment, balancing contradiction, and remembering that peace isn't perfection ~ it's presence with all that you are

There once was a soul who believed it had to choose.

Logic or emotion. Strength or softness. Rest or ambition.

It lived in a tug-of-war, trying to "get it right" ~ splitting itself between shoulds and wants, expectations and needs.

But one still afternoon ~ as the Northern leaves swirled gently in opposing directions, or the Southern sky opened wide with both clouds and sun ~ the soul paused.

And listened.

Not for answers, but for *sound*.

It heard its own breath. Its heartbeat. Its longing. Its truth.

All of it ~ *at once*.

"This isn't a battle," the soul whispered. *"It's a song. My job is not to pick a single note ~ it's to hear the harmony."*

That day, it stopped trying to fix what wasn't broken.

It let itself be whole ~ messy, musical, alive.

Seasonal Awareness:

🌑 In the Northern Hemisphere, as things fall away, inner balance is tested. Let today bring reconciliation between parts of you that seem to disagree.

🌑 In the Southern Hemisphere, new energies rise ~ some conflicting. Allow yourself to harmonize them gently, not force them into agreement.

Archetype of the Day: *The Inner Composer*

This self listens deeply. It doesn't eliminate tension ~ it orchestrates it. It knows that contrast doesn't mean conflict ~ it means *complexity worth honoring.*

Symbols of the Day:

- A tuning fork resonating with a glass of water, unseen balance
- Fluorite, for clarity, integration, and multidimensional wisdom
- The Temperance card, blending opposites, soul equilibrium, divine timing
- A birdsong made of many notes, discordant and beautiful

Reflection Prompts:

— Where am I asking myself to be "either/or" ~ and what if I allowed "both/and"?
— What parts of me are trying to speak at the same time ~ and how can I listen to each with respect?
— What does inner harmony feel like ~ not as silence, but as permission to be whole?

Integration Practice: Harmony Mapping

List three "opposite" qualities or desires in you right now.

Next to each, write how they *can exist together* ~ not by compromising, but by cooperating.

Say:

"I hold all of me with grace. My contradictions do not divide me ~ they define my depth."

Then write:

— "My harmony today sounds like…"
— *"I feel most whole when I…"*

Mantra for Today ~

"I am not torn ~ I am textured. I am not at war ~ I am weaving. My soul sings in layers ~ and I let it rise."

September 19 – The Day of Sacred Pause

A story of intentional stillness, spiritual breath, and learning that stopping is not quitting ~ it's listening

There once was a soul who thought it had to keep going.

One task after another. One healing after another. One transformation after another.

It feared stillness ~ not because it disliked rest, but because it didn't trust what might rise in the silence.

But one day ~ as the Northern air held its breath before the storm, or the Southern breeze softened with quiet invitation ~ the soul stopped.

Not out of exhaustion.

But out of *choice*.

It sat. Not to plan, or process ~ but to *be*.

And in the silence, something whispered:

"You are not behind. You are not broken. You are invited ~ to pause."

Not forever. Just long enough to remember its rhythm. To feel the truth it kept rushing past. To hear what could only be said in stillness.

That day, the soul learned: Stopping was not a failure.

It was a sacred return.

Seasonal Awareness:

🌕 In the Northern Hemisphere, you may feel pulled toward productivity. Let today be the sacred interruption that saves your soul from burnout.

🌑 In the Southern Hemisphere, energy rises. But don't mistake momentum for readiness. Pause ~ so you don't leave yourself behind.

Archetype of the Day: *The Soul Reclaimer*

This self knows when to step back. It listens for fatigue beneath movement. It doesn't wait for collapse to rest ~ it pauses with wisdom, with intention.

Symbols of the Day:

— A rock in the middle of a river, unmoving, steady, whole
— Howlite, for calming, stillness, and spiritual restoration
— The Four of Swords, sacred rest, healing through non-doing

— A comma at the end of a sentence, not an end ~ a breath

Reflection Prompts:

— Where in my life have I been afraid to pause ~ and what truth have I been avoiding in that stillness?
— What would it feel like to stop ~ not as escape, but as sacred return?
— If I were to rest today, what would I finally be able to hear?

Integration Practice: Stillness Invitation

Set a timer for 5 minutes. Do nothing. No agenda. Just sit and breathe.

Say:

"I pause with purpose. I rest as an act of return. I reclaim myself ~ by being still."

Then write:

— *"In the stillness, I felt..."*
— *"What rose when I stopped was..."*

Mantra for Today ~

"I am not lost when I pause. I am found in the space I create. Stillness is not absence ~ it is sacred presence."

September 20 – The Day of Remembered Grace

A story of subtle mercy, inner forgiveness, and learning that what softens you is not weakness ~ but sacred strength

There once was a soul who held itself to impossible standards.

It forgave others with ease ~ but demanded perfection from its own heart.

It relived every mistake. Replayed every hesitation. Rewrote every sentence it wished it had said differently.

But one evening ~ as the Northern sun descended without apology, or the Southern horizon welcomed spring in uneven bloom ~ the soul stumbled upon a memory:

A moment where it had been kind. Gentle. Present. Enough.

And it cried.

Not out of sadness ~ but because it had forgotten that version of itself.

"I don't need to keep punishing the me I once was," the soul whispered. *"She did the best she could ~ and so do I."*

And in that moment, grace arrived.

Not loud. Not earned.

Just remembered.

Seasonal Awareness:

🌘 In the Northern Hemisphere, the changing light brings gentle review. Let grace meet your past today ~ not as correction, but as kindness.

🌒 In the Southern Hemisphere, as energy rises, be careful not to power over your past. Let today be about honoring what brought you here ~ even the imperfect steps.

Archetype of the Day: *The Grace Giver*

This self doesn't seek excuses ~ it seeks understanding. It softens not to bypass pain, but to create space for healing. It remembers that mercy, too, is a form of strength.

Symbols of the Day:

— A hand placed gently over the heart, not to fix ~ but to hold

- Pink calcite, for emotional healing, forgiveness, and compassion
- The Six of Cups, memory, sweetness, emotional reckoning
- A letter written but never sent, no less true for staying with the soul

Reflection Prompts:

- What part of me still feels undeserving of grace ~ and why?
- What memory am I ready to meet again ~ with kindness instead of critique?
- What truth do I know now, that my past self didn't ~ and can I honor her for that?

Integration Practice: Grace Letter

Write a short note to a past version of yourself.

Not to fix. Not to relive. Just to offer grace.

Say:

"You did enough. You were enough. And I carry you now ~ with love, not shame."

Then write:

- "The moment I'm reclaiming today is…"

— *"And the grace I give myself is…"*

¶
¶
¶
¶
¶
¶
¶
¶
¶
¶
¶
¶

Mantra for Today ~

"I do not need to earn grace. I remember it. I return to myself ~ with mercy, with love, with peace."

September 21 - The Day of Equinox Within

A story of inner balance, seasonal reflection, and learning that harmony isn't passive ~ it's a conscious, sacred calibration

There once was a soul who lived in extremes.

All in or all out. All feeling or all control. All silence or all speech.

It thought balance was boring. Or worse ~ fake.

But one luminous day ~ as the Northern sun tipped exactly between light and shadow, or the Southern earth exhaled at the cusp of new bloom ~ the soul stood still.

The world, for a moment, wasn't rushing. Wasn't grasping.

It was just... *even.*

And the soul felt something it hadn't in a long time:

"I am not too much. I am not too little. I am enough ~ as I am, in this moment."

That day, it stopped chasing extremes. Not because they were wrong ~ but because something steadier had been waiting:

Wholeness. The quiet kind. The kind found not in reaching, but in remembering.

Seasonal Awareness:

🌑 In the Northern Hemisphere, the Autumn Equinox nears. Today is an invitation to check your balance ~ not externally, but within.

🌑 In the Southern Hemisphere, the Spring Equinox rises. Let today reflect the harmony of growth and grace ~ of action supported by rest.

Archetype of the Day: *The Inner Balancer*

This self doesn't seek perfection ~ it seeks integration. It doesn't fear the edges ~ but knows when to return to center. It makes space for both stillness and becoming.

Symbols of the Day:

- A stone balanced on another, imperfectly perfect
- Labradorite, for equilibrium, transformation, and soul grounding
- The Justice card, not judgment, but clarity, restoration, and wise balance
- A sun and moon in the same sky, light sharing space with shadow

Reflection Prompts:

- Where in my life have I been swinging too far in one direction ~ and what would balance look like now?
- What would it feel like to stop "fixing" and simply allow myself to return to center?
- How do I know when I am aligned ~ not outside, but in soul rhythm?

Integration Practice: Inner Equinox Check-In

Draw two columns: "What I'm holding too tightly" and "What I'm neglecting."

Breathe deeply. Circle one from each to rebalance.

Say:

"I am not divided. I am dynamic. I am the balance ~ and I return to center with care."

Then write:

- "Today I rebalance by…"
- *"Harmony feels like…"*

Mantra for Today ~

"I am not either/or. I am both/and. I walk in balance ~ not perfectly, but present."

September 22 – The Day of Seasonal Thresholds

A story of crossing consciously, honoring transition, and learning that every doorway holds both memory and becoming

There once was a soul who feared thresholds.

They marked the end of something known ~ and the beginning of something unformed.

Even joyful transitions brought a quiet ache. Because change, however gentle, carried grief.

Then one soft morning ~ as the Northern light shifted toward amber quiet, or the Southern soil opened in wild new greens ~ the soul stood at a literal doorway.

One foot inside. One foot ready to step forward.

And instead of rushing, it paused.

"This matters," it whispered. *"This in-between. This crossing. This moment where I am no longer what I was, but not yet who I will be."*

And so it crossed ~ not out of habit, but with reverence.

Not as escape. Not as arrival.

But as *acknowledgment*.

Because thresholds aren't just passages. They're *portals* ~ to the present version of your becoming.

Seasonal Awareness:

🌑 In the Northern Hemisphere, the threshold into autumn deepens. Let this shift be sacred. Cross with presence ~ not panic.

🌑 In the Southern Hemisphere, spring invites rebirth. But even becoming requires farewell. Honor what is ending as you step forward.

Archetype of the Day: *The Threshold Walker*

This self does not rush from past to future. It pauses. It honors the moment of crossing ~ with presence, clarity, and care. It knows every threshold is an invitation ~ to remember, to release, and to receive.

Symbols of the Day:

— A door left ajar, light spilling through

— Moonstone, for transition, intuition, and sacred movement

- The Two of Pentacles, navigating change, graceful decision, embodied adjustment
- A hand brushing both sides of a doorway, present with both what was and what's next

Reflection Prompts:

- What threshold am I standing at today ~ emotionally, spiritually, or relationally?
- What part of me resists crossing ~ and what part is already moving forward?
- What would it look like to honor this transition instead of rushing past it?

Integration Practice: Crossing Ritual

Stand at an actual doorway. Pause. Name the transition you're in ~ out loud or silently.

Step through with intention.

Say:

"I cross with care. I release what is done. I receive what is rising. I do not skip this threshold ~ I honor it."

Then write:

- "The threshold I crossed today was…"
- *"I felt myself become…"*

Mantra for Today ~

"I do not rush change. I walk through it with reverence. I honor the threshold ~ and trust the becoming."

September 23 – The Day of Light Rebalancing

A story of sacred symmetry, luminous recalibration, and remembering that inner balance is not static ~ it's alive

There once was a soul who didn't realize how tilted it had become.

Busy in one direction. Emotionally weighted in another. Pulled by duty. Pushed by longing.

It called the imbalance "life."

But one luminous day ~ as the Northern world stood at equal parts light and dark, and the Southern earth mirrored it in exact reflection ~ the soul stopped.

The equinox had arrived.

"Day and night are even," it thought. *"So where in me is asking for the same?"*

It didn't strive to "fix" anything. It simply listened.

And in that still moment, something shifted:

Not back to perfection ~ but to presence.

The soul remembered: It isn't the *amount* of light that matters. It's how you *honor* it.

Today was not about balance achieved ~ but balance *remembered*.

Seasonal Awareness:

🌘 In the Northern Hemisphere, today is the Autumn Equinox. The veil thins, the balance deepens. Let today reset your relationship with shadow and light.

🌒 In the Southern Hemisphere, today is the Spring Equinox. Let light return gently. Let your joy come not from noise, but from alignment.

Archetype of the Day: *The Light-Weaver*

This self honors cycles. It doesn't chase brightness or hide from dark. It calibrates. It listens. It *rebalances* ~ not with force, but with grace.

Symbols of the Day:

— A line drawn down the middle of the sky, equal parts gold and indigo
— Ametrine, for blending clarity with calm, light with grounding
— The Justice card, balance, awareness, sacred symmetry

- A scale holding both flame and shadow, neither erased

Reflection Prompts:

- Where in my life have I overcompensated ~ and where am I undernourished?
- How do I respond when light and dark are equal ~ do I welcome the tension, or try to solve it?
- What part of me is ready to recalibrate, not perfectly, but honestly?

Integration Practice: Light & Shadow Journal

Draw a line down a page. Title one side "Light I'm Honoring," the other "Shadow I'm Embracing."

List a few words or images in each.

Say:

"Both are part of me. Neither is wrong. I meet them where they are ~ and bring them into balance."

Then write:

- "What surprised me about today's balance was…"
- *"When I hold both, I feel…"*

¶
¶

Mantra for Today ~

"I do not fear the dark. I do not worship the light. I stand in the balance ~ and I am whole."

September 24 – The Day of Echoed Becoming

A story of reflection without regression, soul loops with new layers, and learning that returning doesn't mean you're lost ~ it means you're ready

There once was a soul who kept circling back.

To patterns. To places. To people and thoughts it thought it had left behind.

At first, it panicked.

"Am I going backward?"

But one clear morning ~ as the Northern leaves fell in familiar spirals, or the Southern blossoms opened in ways they once had before ~ the soul looked closer.

And realized: this wasn't a repeat. This was a *return* ~ but with different eyes. A deeper breath. A clearer heart.

"This is not regression," the soul whispered. *"It's resonance. I'm not back where I started ~ I'm becoming more fully who I am."*

The soul remembered:

Not every spiral is a loop.

Some are a *deepening*.

Seasonal Awareness:

🌑 In the Northern Hemisphere, as autumn echoes previous years, let it remind you of how you've changed ~ not what hasn't.

🌔 In the Southern Hemisphere, spring growth may look familiar. But don't confuse repetition with stagnation ~ this blooming is *new*, because you are.

Archetype of the Day: *The Echoed Self*

This self honors the places it returns to. Not with shame ~ but with awareness. It knows that becoming often means revisiting ~ with gentler hands and stronger roots.

Symbols of the Day:

- A spiral carved in stone, not linear, not stuck
- Lepidolite, for transition, release, and emotional rebalance
- The Wheel of Fortune, cycles, deep shifts, soul timing

- A river bend passed once again, yet everything feels different

Reflection Prompts:

- Where have I returned lately ~ not to repeat, but to realize?
- What part of me feels like it's circling ~ and what wisdom is asking to be claimed there?
- How am I becoming more whole through what I used to avoid?

Integration Practice: Spiral Reflection

Draw a spiral. At the center, write a past version of yourself. On the outer rings, add insights you now carry about that time.

Say:

"I return not to regress ~ but to reclaim. My becoming is not linear. It is layered ~ and it is mine."

Then write:

- "Today I circled back to…"
- "And what I now know is…"

Mantra for Today ~

"I am not repeating. I am revealing. I am the echo ~ and the evolution."

September 25 – The Day of Soul Integrity

A story of living your truth from the inside out, choosing alignment over approval, and remembering that the most sacred yes is the one you give yourself

There once was a soul who knew what it believed ~ but struggled to live it.

It said all the right things. Held the right values. Spoke of authenticity, honesty, and grace.

But its choices didn't always match. Not out of deception ~ but out of fear.

Fear of being too much. Fear of being rejected. Fear of disappointing those who loved a more "convenient" version of it.

Then one clear morning ~ as the Northern light pierced through early haze, or the Southern wind stirred the petals of a blooming truth ~ the soul asked:

"What would it cost to finally live in full alignment with what I know to be true?"

And the answer was gentle:

"Nothing worth keeping."

So the soul began again. Not loudly. Not radically.

But honestly.

It chose not to be perfect ~ but to be *integrated*.

And in that, it felt whole.

Seasonal Awareness:

🌑 In the Northern Hemisphere, inner truth calls for embodiment. Let today be about walking what you know ~ without apology.

🌑 In the Southern Hemisphere, as new energy rises, build it on integrity. Let every yes reflect your soul ~ not just your surroundings.

Archetype of the Day: *The Integrated One*

This self no longer performs authenticity ~ it *lives* it. It doesn't need validation ~ only resonance. It aligns not to prove, but to *honor* its inner truth.

Symbols of the Day:

— A tree growing in perfect light, not tallest ~ but truest

— Carnelian, for courage, authenticity, and creative self-expression
— The King of Swords, wisdom in alignment, sovereign clarity
— A mirror that reflects the soul, not the surface, clear and whole

Reflection Prompts:

— Where in my life am I still shaping myself to fit someone else's comfort?
— What would it look like today to be fully aligned ~ in one small, honest choice?
— What does it feel like when my inner and outer truths finally match?

Integration Practice: Integrity Inventory

List three values that define who you are.

Next to each, write one action ~ however small ~ that brings that value to life today.

Say:

"I live what I believe. I walk with truth ~ not for others, but for myself. My integrity is my peace."

Then write:

- "Today I honored my truth by…"
- "This made me feel…"

Mantra for Today ~

"I do not perform truth. I embody it. I live in soul integrity ~ and that is enough."

September 26 – The Day of Inner Restoration

A story of sacred recovery, whole-self replenishment, and remembering that healing isn't something you earn ~ it's something you allow

There once was a soul who believed it had to be productive to be worthy.

It equated motion with meaning. Busyness with value. Healing with hustle.

So when it tired, it didn't rest ~ it pushed.

Until one quiet evening ~ as the Northern shadows lengthened in early descent, or the Southern blooms rested closed beneath new stars ~ the soul stopped.

Not because it planned to. Because it *had* to.

It lay still. At first feeling guilt, then grief. And finally… grace.

"This rest is not a weakness," the soul whispered. *"It is my body's wisdom. It is my spirit's sanctuary."*

And it listened.

To the ache. To the breath. To the soft rebuilding taking place beneath the silence.

That night, the soul learned:

Healing isn't something you chase. It's something you *receive*.

Seasonal Awareness:

🌑 In the Northern Hemisphere, the turn inward accelerates. Don't resist it. Let today be about sacred stillness ~ and full permission to restore.

🌒 In the Southern Hemisphere, even as energy rises, not all seeds must bloom today. Pause. Let your restoration match your reach.

Archetype of the Day: *The Soul Restorer*

This self reclaims wholeness ~ not by striving, but by surrendering. It knows when to move ~ and when to mend. It trusts that restoration is not passive ~ it is sacred work.

Symbols of the Day:

— A bed unmade in morning light, soft, real, healing
— Rose quartz, for self-compassion, gentle recovery, and emotional warmth

- The Four of Cups, turning inward, emotional renewal, pause for perspective
- A cloud covering the sun briefly, offering shade ~ not obstruction

Reflection Prompts:

- What part of me is tired ~ not because it's lazy, but because it's been carrying too much?
- What would healing look like today if I stopped trying to earn it?
- Where can I restore rather than repair?

Integration Practice: Restoration Permission Slip

Write yourself a short permission slip: "I allow myself to rest, because…"

Read it out loud.

Then say:

"I return to myself ~ not through force, but through care. I am not behind. I am being rebuilt."

Then write:

- "What I gave myself today was…"
- *"And it restored…"*

Mantra for Today ~

"Rest is not a pause in becoming. It is the becoming. I restore myself ~ with love, not guilt."

September 27 – The Day of Soul-Witnessing

A story of sacred observation, compassionate seeing, and learning that healing deepens when we are simply seen without needing to change

There once was a soul who had spent its life trying to be understood.

It explained itself. Overexplained itself. Tried to fit its story into someone else's language.

And still, it felt unseen.

Then one quiet afternoon ~ as the Northern skies held stillness like a mirror, or the Southern winds passed without pulling ~ the soul sat beside another soul.

And that soul said nothing.

No advice. No reaction. No rush.

Just presence.

"I see you," the other whispered. *"You don't have to become anything else to be worthy of this moment."*

And in that space, something softened.

The soul realized ~ it didn't need fixing. It needed *witnessing*.

It didn't need validation. It needed *presence*.

And in being seen ~ wholly, honestly, without edit ~ it began to heal in ways it never had before.

Seasonal Awareness:

🌑 In the Northern Hemisphere, your inner world may need gentle holding. Let today be less about changing ~ more about witnessing what already is.

🌕 In the Southern Hemisphere, even in new growth, be still enough to *see* what's unfolding. Growth deepens through compassionate awareness.

Archetype of the Day: *The Witness*

This self does not fix. It holds. It listens without interrupting. It sees without judgment. And in that, it offers the rarest kind of healing: *presence without pressure*.

Symbols of the Day:

— A mirror with no frame, reflecting what is without altering it

- Rhodonite, for compassion, self-acceptance, and emotional balance
- The Queen of Cups, intuitive presence, deep empathy, sacred stillness
- A quiet nod between two people, wordless, but real

Reflection Prompts:

- What part of me is asking not to be fixed ~ but simply witnessed?
- When was the last time I felt truly seen ~ and what made that possible?
- How can I offer soul-witnessing to myself or someone else today?

Integration Practice: Sacred Mirror Moment

Sit in front of a mirror or close your eyes.

Say:

"I see you. I'm not here to change you. I'm here to stay with you ~ just as you are."

Then write:

"Today, I witnessed myself in…"

"When I let myself be seen, I felt…"

Optionally, offer this same presence to someone else. No fixing. Just witnessing.

¶
¶
¶
¶
¶
¶
¶
¶
¶
¶
¶
¶

Mantra for Today ~

"I am seen. I do not have to earn visibility. I am worthy of being witnessed ~ and I witness with love."

September 28 – The Day of Trusting the Tides

A story of surrender, timing, and learning that life moves in rhythms that carry us ~ even when we can't see where they're leading

There once was a soul who tried to control everything.

It made plans. Built structures. Held on tightly ~ even when the tide had long since shifted.

Because letting go felt like failure. And surrender felt like floating with no anchor.

But one dusk ~ as the Northern waves rolled in with unhurried certainty, or the Southern ocean sighed against the early bloom of sand ~ the soul stood at the water's edge.

The tide moved.

It hadn't asked permission. It didn't explain.

It just *moved*.

And the soul saw that it wasn't random. It was *rhythmic*. It returned.

"I don't have to push this ocean," the soul whispered. *"I only need to trust that it knows how to carry me."*

And for the first time, the soul loosened its grip.

Not in defeat ~ but in trust.

Because what carries you is not chaos ~ it's current.

Seasonal Awareness:

🌑 In the Northern Hemisphere, let the slow turn of the season teach you to trust timing. Don't resist the retreat ~ let the ebb show you your rhythm.

🌒 In the Southern Hemisphere, spring rushes in. But let the tide rise in its own time. You don't have to force bloom ~ it comes with the pull of readiness.

Archetype of the Day: *The Tidal Soul*

This self flows. It does not fight timing. It doesn't cling to outcomes. It surrenders ~ not as a loss, but as alignment.

It lets the tide carry what must go, and bring back what belongs.

Symbols of the Day:

- A message in a bottle, carried not by speed ~ but by trust
- Aquamarine, for flow, peace, and emotional truth

- The Moon card, intuition, tides, subconscious movement
- A boat anchored but not tethered, allowed to rise and fall freely

Reflection Prompts:

- Where am I resisting a natural shift, because I fear losing control?
- What would it look like today to trust the tide ~ not as chaos, but as timing?
- How do I know when it's time to hold ~ and when it's time to release?

Integration Practice: Tidal Visualization

Close your eyes. Imagine a gentle tide pulling out, then returning.

Name one thing you're ready to let go of ~ and one thing you're ready to allow in.

Say:

"I trust the timing. I trust the return. I am moved, not by force ~ but by faith."

Then write:

- "What I released to the tide was…"

— *"What I welcome with the next wave is…"*

Mantra for Today ~

"I surrender to rhythm. I do not rush the sea. I trust the tide ~ and the part of me it brings home."

September 29 – The Day of Sacred Threads

A story of hidden connections, quiet continuity, and learning that nothing meaningful is ever truly lost ~ it's woven deeper than you think

There once was a soul who thought it had come undone.

So many beginnings that never ended. So many threads pulled loose. So many relationships, ideas, and paths that never quite found their finish.

It looked back and saw fray.

But one golden morning ~ as the Northern light softened into harvest hues, or the Southern air buzzed with emerging life ~ the soul traced one memory.

A small kindness. A quiet decision. An old journal entry.

And it noticed ~ the thread hadn't broken. It had simply disappeared *beneath* for a while, only to surface again ~ *right here*.

"It's all connected," the soul whispered. *"Even the parts I thought I lost ~ they were holding me the whole time."*

And with that, the soul stopped chasing neatness. Stopped trying to make the story symmetrical.

It chose instead to honor the thread. Not for where it led ~ but for what it held.

Seasonal Awareness:

🌘 In the Northern Hemisphere, as endings approach, today is a reminder that the threads of your life are never wasted. They are being woven.

🌑 In the Southern Hemisphere, as life reawakens, recognize that what begins now may be rooted in a thread you once thought had ended.

Archetype of the Day: *The Weaver*

This self honors continuity, not clarity. It follows what is felt ~ not always seen. It trusts that the soul's story is stitched in invisible gold.

Nothing is random. Everything is thread.

Symbols of the Day:

— A loom mid-weave, threads tangled, but strong
— Garnet, for grounding, connection, and ancestral memory

- The World card, completion, unity, unseen cycles completing themselves
- A bracelet made from many frayed fibers, beautiful in its complexity

Reflection Prompts:

- What thread from my past is showing up again now ~ not to repeat, but to reconnect?
- Where have I dismissed something as "unfinished" that is still deeply holding me?
- What sacred threads have I woven ~ even without knowing it?

Integration Practice: Thread Trace

Write down five meaningful moments from your life, across time. Look for the invisible thread between them.

Say:

"Nothing I've lived is wasted. Every thread matters. I am stitched into meaning ~ even when I cannot see the full pattern."

Then write:

- "The thread I follow today is…"
- *"It connects me to…"*

Mantra for Today ~

"I am not unravelling. I am weaving. My life is held by sacred threads ~ seen and unseen."

September 30 – The Day of Integration

A story of weaving wholeness, harvesting wisdom, and remembering that everything you've lived belongs ~ especially the parts you almost left behind

There once was a soul who wanted closure.

Not because it was broken ~ but because it was ready to make sense of everything it had carried.

The healing. The heartbreak. The pieces that never seemed to fit.

It didn't want a clean ending ~ it wanted meaning.

Then one golden evening ~ as the Northern trees rustled with the final voice of autumn's entrance, or the Southern dusk settled warm upon the skin of new leaves ~ the soul sat down and gathered everything.

Its joy. Its sorrow. Its failures, softness, doubt, and spark.

And instead of sorting it into "good" and "bad," it simply whispered:

"All of this… is me. All of it belongs."

And the moment it said that ~ the pieces stopped fighting. They folded into each other. And the soul felt, for the first time in a long time, not "fixed"… but *whole*.

Seasonal Awareness:

◍ In the Northern Hemisphere, the end of harvest season invites deep integration. Let what you've learned settle fully into your being.

◐ In the Southern Hemisphere, as life returns, integrate gently. Bring forward what is true ~ not what is urgent. Let the whole of you rise.

Archetype of the Day: *The Integrator*

This self welcomes what was scattered. It does not force cohesion ~ it *allows* it. It knows that wisdom is not found in perfection, but in presence with the *whole self*.

Symbols of the Day:

— A bundle wrapped in soft cloth, containing many pieces ~ all sacred

— Unakite, for integration, gentle transformation, emotional acceptance

— The Temperance card, alchemy, balance, divine blending

- A bowl filled with different fruits of the season, imperfect, abundant

Reflection Prompts:

- What part of me have I tried to leave behind ~ and is now asking to be welcomed back?
- What wisdom have I harvested from the contradictions, the chaos, the change?
- How does it feel to be whole ~ not polished, but present?

Integration Practice: Wholeness Reflection

Write down three parts of yourself you once tried to change, reject, or ignore. Next to each, write how that part has helped you grow.

Say:

"I am not a collection of mistakes and triumphs. I am a living whole. And I integrate all that I've lived ~ with reverence."

Then write:

- *"Today, I reclaim…"*
- *"I honor this part of me because…"*

Mantra for Today ~

"I am not a puzzle to solve. I am a story to honor. I am whole ~ and I begin again from here."

September Reflection

Integration of the Deep Waters: Wholeness, Witness, and Return

You've walked through shadows. You've floated in mystery. You've touched sorrow, tenderness, silence, and strength ~ all without needing to resolve them.

Volume 3, *Unveiling the Unknown*, has not been about answers.

It has been about becoming brave enough to ask the questions ~ and sit with what arises.

This month has been water: not always calm, not always clear, but always capable of carrying you deeper into yourself.

What You've Lived Through This Month

- ✔ You've learned to trust tides, not timelines.
- ✔ You've opened without force and closed without collapse.
- ✔ You've welcomed silence as a teacher.
- ✔ You've practiced sacred pauses and soft boundaries.
- ✔ You've practiced devotional presence.
- ✔ You've begun to witness yourself ~ fully, gently, honestly.

Whether you felt that every day or missed pages along the way, what matters is this:

You stayed. You kept coming back. You kept listening.

Journal Prompts for Reflection:

Take a moment to sit with these questions. Let your responses rise without pressure.

— What part of myself feels more whole after this month?

— Which day's message stayed with me ~ or echoed into my choices?

— What did I unearth that I hadn't made space to feel before?

— How has my relationship with the unknown changed ~ even subtly?

Practices to Carry Forward:

⊚ The Spiral Practice: Choose one day from this month. Re-read it. Now write how you would respond to that same entry today. What's shifted? What's stayed?

❁ The Gentle Return: Keep one mantra from this month visible ~ on your mirror, your phone, or beside your bed. Let it become a soft tether when the world feels too loud.

✸ The Trust Map: Draw a circle. Label it "The Unknown." Around it, write all the ways you've learned to trust what you cannot see. Let this be your map for the days ahead.

Final Mantra for September

"I do not need certainty to be whole. I walk with what is real ~ not resolved. I am the witness, the wave, and the return. I am home ~ within myself."

Notes

Your Depth Has Carried You...

You made it.

You've journeyed through *Unveiling the Unknown* ~ not by force, but by surrender.

For 92 days, you've floated through emotion, moved with mystery, and softened into the sacred truth beneath the surface.

- You've trusted tides instead of timelines.
- You've allowed what was hidden to rise gently.
- You've embraced the quiet unravelling of who you thought you had to be.

But now... there's a different current forming.

A shift in pressure.

A shimmer below the waterline.

A question rising from somewhere deep:

- "What will I do with the truth I've found?"

That's where Volume 4 ~ *Light in the Layers* begins. The next 91 days are not about more depth ~ they are about integration. About claiming clarity without perfection. About rising with all that you've remembered and learning how to live from your wholeness.

- If Volume 1 taught you how to arrive
- If Volume 2 helped you open
- And Volume 3 showed you how to surrender and see...

Then Volume 4 will guide you in becoming ~ with wisdom, with perspective, with light.

This is your season to return from the waters ~ not to leave them behind, but to carry what they gave you into the world.

So take one more breath. Dry your hands. Look toward the horizon. And step into what comes next ~ clearer, fuller, and ready to live the truth that surfaced when you stopped searching and started listening.

You're not leaving the depths. You're bringing their light with you.

www.ingramcontent.com/pod-product-compliance
Lightning Source LLC
LaVergne TN
LVHW020925090426
835512LV00020B/3208